The Stagnant Civilization

The Stagnant Civilization

an Exercise in Hermeneutics

Edward Lyons

iUniverse, Inc.
New York   Bloomington

The Stagnant Civilization
an Exercise in Hermeneutics

iUniverse books may be ordered through booksellers or by contacting:

iUniverse
1663 Liberty Drive
Bloomington, IN 47403
www.iuniverse.com
1-800-Authors (1-800-288-4677)

ISBN: 978-1-4401-4298-7 (pbk)
ISBN: 978-1-4401-4297-0 (ebk)

Printed in the United States of America

iUniverse rev. date: 6/16/2009

"Qu' est-ce que la littérature?"
Interpretability in the Speculative Exercise

This will not have been written so much as orchestrated through the systematic juxtaposition of discontinuous texts. In the critical crucible of Faulknerian studies, the distinction between literature and literary criticism has been rendered problematic. This distinction finds a clear and concise utterance in Clcanth Brooks' insight, "there is a sense in which paradox is the language inevitable and appropriate to poetry. It is the scientist whose truth requires a language purged of every trace of paradox; apparently the truth which the poet utters can be approached only in terms of paradox" *(The Well Wrought Urn* 3). However, John T. Irwin, in the Introduction to his watershed meditation on Faulkner, *Doubling and Incest/Repetition and Revenge,* observes in regard to the application of psychoanalysis to literature, "In juxtaposing Faulkner and Freud or Faulkner and Nietzsche, my aim was not to explain or reduce or simplify Faulkner's novels but to make them more problematic, richer and more complex. At the same time I realized that the reciprocal nature of such a juxtaposition would render the works of Freud and Nietzsche more problematic as well" (2). This statement implies that paradox is the language of not only literature but of criticism, science, and philosophy as well, an implication which is reflected in the increasing tendency of critics to treat Faulknerian texts as discourse, using the poetic and prosaic categories more or less interchangeably. Both Brooks and Irwin confer a validity on the language of the imagination, but for Brooks and the New Critical position, this validity is confined to the sphere of literature, which is divorced from the scientific/critical mode of truth, whereas Irwin adopts as critical method

to create an imaginative space in which there could be a superposition or interpenetration of every element by every other element, a space in which every element could be simultaneously folded into every other element. And the reason for this is that in the structure it is not simply a case of every element simultaneously interacting with every other element, but rather that by that simultaneous in-

1

teraction the elements mutually create one another, mutually constitute themselves *as elements in a holistic structure* " *(7)*.

Hence, criticism is itself a kind of fiction, by which intertextual relationships reveal themselves through the play of free association as experienced by the reader.

Irwin chooses to read Faulkner in Juxtaposition with Freud and Nietzsche because "they were writers who addressed themselves to many of the same questions, and that at numerous points their works form imaginative analogues to one another." (2-3). This points to a methodology which is based on metaphor, and Irwin states that in the composition of *Doubling and Incest,* "I was unconsciously guided by work I had done earlier on Hart Crane's 'logic of metaphor', -- specifically, on the way in which Crane dissolves syntax in order to create within the poem a fluid linguistic medium in which the reader is led to manipulate metaphoric vehicles in a kind of controlled free association" (8). Metaphor, then, may be assumed to constitute a logically valid premise, whether it follow the model of simile, as in Irwin's statement "the unconscious is structured *like* language" (3, emphasis mine), a predicated model, as in Norman 0. Brown's statement "Love *is* all fire" (Love's Body 179, emphasis mine), or an unpredicated model, again drawing from Brown, "violent eruption, volcanism; the patient becomes violent as he wakes up" (LB 180). This last model contains the most radical implications for conventional syntax: the pause, the semicolon, the silence, acts in lieu of the absent verb. As John T. Matthews asserts, "The 'pure' space of silence is in fact already a syntactical unit, part of the system of articulated differences that constitutes writing" (42). In *Love's Body,* Norman 0. Brown discovers the extreme of this type of syntax, adopting a fractured grammar within an aphoristic format: "Broken flesh, broken mind, broken speech. Truth, a broken body: fragments or aphorisms; as opposed to systematic form or methods: 'Aphorisms, representing a knowledge broken, do invite the mind to inquire farther; whereas methods, carrying the show of a total, do secure men, as if they were at farthest" (188, citing also Bacon). Truth reveals itself in the blank space between the juxtaposed texts, which group themselves around the structure of the unpredicated metaphor.

What I grapple toward through these generalizations is the articulation of a theoretical basis for the manner in which I have chosen to approach William Faulkner's novel *Absalom, Absalom!*, a novel which has proven to be notoriously frustrating when approached from a more conventional critical perspective. But criticism of the novel from Irwin on has been amazingly rich, and has carried broad implications on a number of important critical and philosophical issues. It demands an interdisciplinary and intertextual approach, and is therefore inaccessible to the New Critical position, which views the literary text as a self-contained unit. The technical concepts of conventional criticism: plot, character, theme, etc., are inadequate in interpreting a novel in which time itself is suspended and ego is dissolved in a maze of voices occupying a past and present that are linked by an extensive web of unconscious interconnections, and these voices are motivated by forces which the New Criticism can only guess at.

The literary work exists within a larger context, and *Absalom, Absalom!* is shown to be interconnected with psychoanalysis (Irwin), Historiography (Rollyson), French Poststructural theory (Matthews), Colloquial resources viewed from a sociohistorical perspective (Sundquist), Rhetorical Analysis (Snead), and Dramaturgy (Wadlington). Each reader of the novel must grapple with the Derridaean question "qu' est-ce que la littérature?" (La dissemination 203), and the result of this struggle is a criticism which, far from having the purely Castalian relevance of the New Criticism, engages extremely vital questions. To single out an example of this, Eric J. Sundquist, in *Faulkner: A House Divided* examines the issue of racism, and in so doing analyses the riddle of a sphinx that has ravaged America for three centuries. In tracing the heart of the problem to the sexual amalgamation between slaveholder and slave, and describing the impact this had on family life in the South, Sundquist opens new issues concerning the structure of the unconscious which are not treated in the psychoanalytic literature.

There is a pure space, a silence, generated by the collision of discontinuous texts. This silence is the verb which mediates the subject and the object of the metaphor, which may be a pair of citations from previously written texts. The Being of the metaphor reveals itself in this silence, and the degree of harmony and resonance, apprehended by the imagination of the reader, is the factor which determines the validity of the metaphoric structure. There is a sense in which this exercise resembles a musical composition, in which the tone of a chapter may be governed by a series of epigraphs set over and against it, and in which long passages consist of multiple series of deliberately selected citations from Faulkner, from Brown, and from others, connected by little or no original commentary.

I have sought to develop a means of describing the archetypal quality of *Absalom*. In my initial reading of the novel I was impressed not so much by its strangeness as by its familiarity. It is a novel of instincts, of Eros and Thanatos in conflict. It is about the instinctual bonding of men into the family (Sutpen), the community (Yoknapatawpha), and the nation (America), and about the instinct which undermines these bonds, imposing divisions within the family (Master/Slave), the community (racial segregation, "Niggertown"), and the nation (Civil War). What we read in *Absalom* are the repressed memories of America itself; the novel is structured like a dream dreamt by a whole society.

Another striking feature of *Absalom* is the prominence of its economic vision. The society it presents is inhabited by the poor who are locked in the power of the privileged and wealthy, in a plantation economy in which men are owned by other men. The Will to Power which motivates the planter is real; equally real are the injustice of the system and the suffering of those who are oppressed by it. The reader, then, is confronted with the question of the dichotomous rubrics of symbolism and realism. Is *Absalom* a novel of the subjective visions of its voices, or of the objective reality of labor and production, wealth and poverty? To choose either approach to the exclusion of the other is to read two very different novels, with both being incomplete and neither being adequate.

I have chosen Norman 0. Brown's psychoanalytic interpretation of history, contained in his books *Life Against Death* (1959) and *Love's Body* (1966) as the chief text with which to juxtapose Faulkner, because these works provide a theoretical framework that bridges the interior world of myth and symbol with the world of the socio-economist in a way which reveals the hidden interconnections between them, as well as accounting for the origins of both as phenomena. Brown explores the concept of sublimation, which is never clearly defined in the writings of the psychoanalysts, as a bridge between the study of individual neurosis and the study of culture. In *Life Against Death,* he argues that all cultural achievements, such as art and religion, science and technology, commerce and urbanization, come about through the deflection of repressed libidinal energy away from those sexual organizations developed during infancy, i.e., the oral, the anal, and the phallic. The development of these is the gradual consequence of the child's anxiety over separation from the mother, experienced during the trauma of birth and repeated throughout infanthood and the process of nursing. The infant experiences the womb and the breast as part of its own narcissistic ego, which is omnipotent; separation from these is experienced as a variety of death. In this fashion, the Freudian instincts, Eros and Death, harmoniously present throughout nature, are in the human animal set against each other, as anxiety progressively causes the Death Instinct to be repressed. The polymorphously perverse body, the infantile body throughout which the libido is evenly distributed so that every part is a source of pleasure, evolves into the body ruled by the sexual organizations, in which the libido is concentrated in the oral, anal, and genital zones. The entire body desires a return to the state in which it existed before birth, but the sexually organized body is, as Brown tells in *Love's Body,* a *corporation,* which the penis rules as Chief Executive Officer, the member who may alone enjoy the privilege of sexual intercourse.

Through the castration complex, the sexual organizations become mutually identified through a process which Ferenczi calls "the amphimixis of erotisms" (cited in ED 290). The Child, faced with the threat of death as punishment for his incestuous desire for the mother, renounces the phallus in order to save the rest of the body. The phallus, having become disjoined, becomes identified with that first object to separate from his body, the feces, as well as the mother's breast which withdrew at the time of weaning, and himself, who was torn loose from the mother during birth. The psychological link between these objects is the common experience of separation, and together they comprise the series of organizations that make up the neurotic body, the body in flight from, and bent on conquering, death. But in awarding the lost realm of Eros primacy over Death, the neurotic individual paradoxically allows

Death to dominate Eros. The root of the problem, summarized here, is essentially the psychoanalytic ground which Irwin covers in *Doubling and Incest.* Irwin brilliantly explores the castration complex resulting from the Oedipal project in the case of Quentin Compson, revealing their presence behind the events of the summer of 1909 described in The *Sound and the Fury,* and how in *Absalom* Quentin projects onto the Sutpen story. In fact there is a point at which Brown and Irwin, each pursuing his own ends, virtually echo each other in their respective summaries of Freud's book *Beyond the Pleasure Principle,* which speculates on the existence and origin of the Death Instinct as a compulsion to repeat the inorganic state which precedes life, to repeat a state of utter rest. The repetition compulsion is ultimately the compulsion to repeat this inactive state, a repetition which occurs only in death.

But Brown extends the application of this interpretation of the structure of individual neurosis to the study of the broader problem of culture, understanding that the structure of society itself is essentially neurotic. Culture is the creation of the process of sublimation, by which the unconscious desires of the sexually organized libido are transferred onto the conscious, external world. That is, individually and collectively, neurotic man attempts to actualize his inner fantasies by recreating them in the real world. The repressed desires and fantasies of the unconscious express themselves in the form of a God, a Temple, a City, a Bank, a Monument. Sublimation is the process which links the life of the lower parts of the body with the higher life of the mind; for Brown, bodily activity is the unconscious link between religious and economic activity. The result of his study is a comprehensive *weltanschauung* which is profoundly interdisciplinary, drawing on the fields of psychology, anthropology, theology and scripture, literary criticism, architecture, economics and philosophy, to list a few of the more distinguishable fields he draws on in supporting and enlarging his position. This work is heavily supported by an encyclopedic knowledge of the major psychoanalysts: he is able to compare theoretical positions taken by Ferenczi, Jones, Glover, Rank, Klein, Fromm, Reich, and Roheim, and is thoroughly familiar with the full range of the Freudian texts. Employing a writer such as Brown as a textual referent is to access an immense intertextual network: the bibliography of *Life Against Death* lists a staggering 153 authors, and a persistent quirk encountered in commenting on Brown is the citation within the citation. Brown often establishes a crucial point by using an analogy to his thought provided by means of a direct quote from some other author, so that to cite Brown is often to cite Ferenczi or Frazer, Keynes or Kierkegaard, Lukacs or Luther, Marx or Mumford, Tillich or Trilling, Whitehead or Wittgenstein. Clearly, Brown writes out of an encyclopedic knowledge not only of psychoanalysis, but of English and Modern European Literatures, and the entire tradition of Western Philosophy, and an extensive knowledge of a host of other disciplines. And *Love's Body* contributes more than a few new titles to the list! This volume contains a note of acknowledgement which concludes with the words

> Thanks to the publishers, a page has been designed which, by including references in the body of the text, is a perpetual acknowledgement of my indebtedness to a very great company, both living and dead: my authorities, my authors (iii).

Like Quentin Compson, Norman O. Brown is a vast hall of ghostly voices, and his strange intellectual odyssey ends in fragmentation and chaos, but a chaos which is charged with meaning and full of the vision of redemption. Brown's work is a rigorously reasoned critique of reality that achieves, in the closing chapters of *Love's Body,* a condition of pure mysticism.

In *Life Against Death* , the critique of history is concerned primarily with the sublimation of anal erotism and the manifestations of this in human culture. After devoting half of his volume to laying the theoretical groundwork, Brown presents the "Studies in Anality" section, which commences with the interpretation of the work of Jonathan Swift in a chapter titled "The Excremental Vision." He begins by discrediting those critics who disparage Swift on the basis of the novelist's grossly scatological writings, and those who would turn psychoanalysis against the author in a way which distracts the reader and focuses attention on the neurotic composition of the author's own personality. Instead, Brown methodically follows Swift's stream of scatological imagery to the utmost in order to reveal the vision of mankind that Swift thereby presents: a vision of man as essentially a filthy creature. Brown next applies the scatological reading to the writings of Martin Luther in a chapter titled "The Protestant Era." It is noted here that Luther received the doctrine of Justification by Faith Through Grace, which is central to the Protestant scheme of salvation, while taking a bowel movement in the tower of a monastery (202). Brown interprets the Protestant Reformation as a profound change in human consciousness with the coming awareness that sublimation, or Good Works, is insufficient to achieve salvation, that the Devil is the lord of this world and this world is utterly filthy, and that in this life and this body, filth cannot be transcended. Therefore the Christian must live in the midst of filth and can in this life perform only the Devil's work, while relying on the Grace of God as the sole means of attaining a pure life in the world to come. It is this mode of consciousness, which swept Europe at the end of the Middle Ages, that allowed the birth of capitalism to take place.

The hidden connection between the sacred and the secular is the topic of *Life Against Death*'s most extensive chapter, "Filthy Lucre." Here, the accumulation of money is viewed as the accumulation of symbolic feces, and the irrational and sacred character of economic activity is developed through discussion of the archaic economy of primitive society up through late capitalism with its awesome technology and the vast scope of its urbanization. This is the ultimate outcome of sublimation: the total loss of nature, massive accumulations of stone, a world in which men are governed by money, in which the general mood is one of profound discontent, and the repressed Death Instinct, from which we fled so frantically, rules over all of life. At the Extremes of Sublimation lies the Stagnant Civilization.

Life Against Death concludes with the chapter "The Resurrection of the Body," which sketches out an eschatology which is brought to fruition in *Love's Body*. En Route, the latter volume examines the psychoanalytic underpinnings of democracy in terms of Freud's myth of the primal horde, and constructs a genealogy which originates with the Primal Scene, in which the child, viewing the parents in coitus, becomes the primal audience, descending through the tragic theater of the Greeks, the theater of Roman Jurisprudence, the national theater of monarchy, and finally, the modern political arena.

William Faulkner's name is a significant omission from the Brownian bibliography; this cannot be for lack of familiarity with recent American fiction, for Jack Kerouac is represented here. This omission becomes especially striking when one regards the host of major thinkers whom Brown acknowledges. Shakespeare and Faulkner are the two most important writers to be excluded. But the systematic juxtaposition of Brown and Faulkner produces an intertextual space filled with an apparently infinite, but possibly finite, number of oscillations. Brown reveals the neurotic structure of history; Faulkner produces a novel which reveals an obsession with history among a series of narrative voices who carry the dead burden of the past. *Absalom, Absalom!* is a novel in which Protestantism and capitalism are ubiquitous and closely interrelated, in which wealth is endlessly accumulated in a dynastic quest for immortality. That the material covered by Brown pervades what is most striking and memorable in Faulkner is the reason why so much of this exercise is concerned with describing the structure of the silence that inhabits the space between the two texts. In this exercise, the reading of Faulkner is governed by a consciousness conditioned by the Brownian paradigm. There is no central thesis which is systematically argued; instead, the exercise discovers its themes as it develops, in this way producing a body of insights from which provisional conclusions might be drawn. "The Will to a system is a lack of integrity," says Nietzsche *(Twilight of the Idols* 470), and Brown: "systematic form attempts to evade the necessity of death in the life of the mind as of the body: it has immortal longings in it, and so it remains dead" (LB 188). To work with an author like Brown in an integrated manner is to work within the parameters of the Brownian moral imperative; it is necessary to create a discourse that lets in the silence (LB 190); that is, to treat all text as *living word.* And the texts we have chosen to treat are those which exert a powerful influence over the life of the intellect, texts that can and must interact within the living imagination. It is this interaction which is documented by this exercise, and not the adherence to any arbitrary prejudice, pinned down in a sequence of demonstrable, though meaningless truths. Literary criticism cannot continually exist in an environment which is intellectually sterile, and detached from all other modes of signification, and self-contained within a limited academic discipline. Literary criticism, as a viable mode of knowledge, must confront those issues which are essential to the living, and those conditions under which men and women continue to suffer, as well as those toward which they direct their dearest hopes. And Faulknerian criticism since Irwin has shown, in a preliminary way, that this is possible.

In order to advance this exercise to its end, it is often necessary to invoke an alternative paradigm, which, though using different terms, complements the Brownian. For this, I have chosen to look to Nietzsche. Unlike Irwin, who finds his models in the mature Nietzsche of *Zarathustra,* I find the referential framework which suits my particular needs in his first work, *The Birth of Tragedy,* specifically, in the model of the Apollonian/Dionysian conflict. This model integrates well with the texts we have already opened; Brown sets the precedent by titling the last chapter in his discussion of sublimation "Apollo and Dionysus." For Brown, Apollo is a metaphor for the process of sublimation; both cast the pleasant veil of illusion over the raw instincts, thus making life bearable; Dionysus is the life of the body, the dancer and the dance inseparable, the unsublimated, unrepressed, unneurotic ego (LD 172-76).

Nietzsche's Apollo is the god of the plastic arts, the painter of the image, the carver of the stone, the patron of the Sutpen graveyard. Apollo rules over the realm of dreams, the fair illusion. He is the bright god, the bringer of rational reason, the sun god, the god of the tranquil limit, the *principium individuationis.* Divisions, facades, walls, categories, distinctions: these are the tools with which Apollo constructs the illusion, the world seen from afar, through the eye. Apollo is the lord of the spectator.

Opposed to Apollo stands Dionysus, the drunken god, the god who tears the curtain and participates in the unbearable reality which lies beyond. He is the patron of music: not the tranquil, regular, architecturally structured music of the Apollonian, but the wild, dissonant, disturbing music that lacks all capacity to lie. Dionysus throws back the soothing veil, abrogates all limits, demolishes all walls. To experience Dionysus is to experience the unity of all nature, and to participate in this unity, to touch it, to taste it, and to become intimate with the agony and ecstasy of the dissolution of the individual consciousness. Apollo is honored by civilization, whose instincts are repressed and harnessed; Dionysus is honored by the revelers of the orgy. Apollo is consciousness among the walls of the city; Dionysus is naked in the fields and forests who are unconscious of themselves as such. Apollo is clarity and distinction; Dionysus is contradiction and pain.

The stream of the voices in *Absalom,* the voices that make up the total narration, the voices of Rosa and Mr. Compson, of Quentin and Shreve, of General Compson and Judith and Charles Bon, resembles Nietzsche's conception of the tragic chorus, the collective voice of the devotees of the god, "a chorus of the transformed, who have forgotten their civic past and social rank, who have become timeless of their god and live outside all social spheres" (BT 56). For the chorus, the stage *is* reality, and the masked figure who rises in their midst through the power of their incantation is the actual god. *Absalom's* narrators do not forget their social rank, but its meaning ebbs inexorably away as through the power of their blended voiced they create and behold Thomas Sutpen. This is why the voices of the several narrators are continuous, and not readily distinguished from one another by marks of rhetorical individuality as in *The Sound and the Fury.* But in *Absalom,* the narrator is also by turns The spectator, projecting himself onto the action on the stage, viewing with the eye the images that pass before him, the images of the Apollonian dream.

Behind this astonished viewing stands the essentially tragic structure of the Primal Scene, in which the child, encountering the sight of the parents engaged in coitus, becomes frozen with fear and excitement and fascination. These are the emotions that grip Quentin as he beholds the actors in the Sutpen drama, paralyzing him, robbing him of the ability to voice his own part in the drama. The Primal Scene is the event which shatters the universal brotherhood of Dionysian man, polarizing us into actor and audience. In *Reading Faulknerian Tragedy,* Warwick Wadlington suggests that *human being* is created through the continual repetitive performance of a multitude of scripts within the theater of culture (30-34; Cf. LD 287). But the spectator speaks no script; within the theater the spectator is a *nonperson,* incapable of the Brownian sublimation by which the *person* is created. To be paralyzed in an encounter with the Primal Scene is to undergo the shattering of individual consciousness, to experience the Dionysian terror of Oedipus (BT 60-61).

The deconstruction of the Apollonian/Dionysian dualism reveals nothing so much as its inherent instability. The two elements are locked in a state of battle, in which each is distinguishable but not separable from the other. Thus this dualism constitutes a highly fluid paradigm having highly fluid boundaries, which is uniquely suited to charting the play of Faulkner's highly fluid novel. It is a mythic referent, set alongside and complementary to, Brown's theoretical referent.

It is impossible to complete the survey of our preliminary assumptions, indeed our prejudices, without confronting the problem of racism and its profound effect of the play of the unconscious. While this exercise makes no specific focus of the problem, it nevertheless occupies a deeply integral position in our understanding of the intertextual space we seek to examine. Perhaps the most comprehensive treatment of the problem in reference to *Absalom* is Regine Robin's contribution to Viola Sachs' anthology *Le Blanc* a *le Noir chez Melville et Faulkner*. This highly eclectic reading presumes an anti-Dionysian structure for racism as a phenomenon; the white man's tendency is to view the black man as a thing or an abstraction, a reflexive process which destroys the psychological life of its practitioner: "In the following pages of our analysis,. we will attempt to constantly underline the endemic malady which undermines Sutpen's propriety and relegates every inhabitant to An effective aridity, a psychic desert . . . a plethora of images revolves around a vocabulary suggesting sterility, obscurity, and negation of life (72-4. translation mine). The excrementality of this situation is not lost of Robin; the Sutpen Design is noted as the mansion built from mud (72, 74 footnote 10). The latter note also cites a source (Joel Kovel, *White Racism: A Psychohistory*), which integrates the black man into the equation of the amphimixis of erotisms (Cf. LD 288-89): the black man is identified with the father, child, body, penis, feces, and thing, and the excremental, arid state in which the racist lives is the return of the repressed original exploitation of the black.

Eric Sundquist, in *Faulkner: The House Divided,* discusses even stranger fantasies which underlie the racist view, fantasies which are based in the sexual reality of the time of slavery. Here, the primal event is shadowed by the sexual relations between the white owner, the father of the plantation, and his female slaves. The sexual act becomes alienated from itself as a logical consequence of the radical abstraction of the black man as property. Echoing a figure which underlies *Absalom*, Sundquist formulates the dilemma thusly: "How without intense moral and psychological convulsions, could the South keep slaves as beasts and lovers alike? And what, then, to do with the children who so vividly embodied these contradictory attitudes in one blasphemous image?" (98). One response is the projection of the transgression onto a perceived desire for the white woman onto the black man. This fantasy creates what Robin calls "la femme blanche du Sud," and demands that she be protected from the feared beast, the monstrous double. This myth restricts and reduces all possibility for women by reducing them to an abstraction as well. In negating another we negate ourselves; this alienation is reflected in the ambivalence toward her sexuality that this view imposes on every woman: there is the wedding veil and Rosa's "dreamy panoply of surrender"; there is also the excremental aspect of sexuality, the loathsomeness of Sutpen's outrageous proposal. Caroline and Candace Compson symbolize the whole range of possible sexual expression open to Southern Womanhood: repression and barrenness, promiscuity and public shame.

The fantastic Negro clearly is present in every figure in the most intimate levels of the unconscious:

> the admixture of blood and identity when incest is involved with, and ultimately paired with, miscegenation. It is exactly the nature of the crisis that leads the South into Civil War (and the entire nation into a prolonged act of fratricide) that it grows out of a 'monstrous' system in which, at the simplest level, slaves both were and were not human beings, and in which at a more significant level for our purposes, sexual violence could issue in a state of simultaneous differentiation and nondifferentiation between father and son or brother and brother. (One should add that the same crisis prevails and, as we have seen, is furthered in the paradoxical relationships among husbands, wives, mothers and daughters) the slave father whose "son" was not his son, and particularly the slave son who

had, therefore, no father at all stand in the most painful roles in this reciprocal tragedy (Sundquist 125).

At this level, racism and incest combine into what becomes the central Faulknerian problematic, the social reality of a culture which is radically alienated from itself. The effect of the abolition of slavery is the transformation of "slave" and "property" into a new abstraction, "nigger", a free agent operating at random, a lascivious beast preying upon the Southern Woman. This underlying anxiety is repressed all the more intensely, the effect of which manifests itself as the social reality of Jim Crow, which perpetuates itself by repeating what Snead schematizes as a script consisting of:

> the fear of *merging,* or loss of identity through synergistic union with the other, leads to the wish to use racial purification as a separating strategy against difference; (2) *marking,* or supplying physically significant (usually visual) characteristics with internal value equivalents, sharpening by visual antithesis their conceptual utility; (3) *spatial and conceptual separation,* often facilitated through unequal verbal substitutions that tend to omit and distance a subordinate class from realms of value and esteem; (4) *repetition,* or pleonastic reinforcement of these antitheses in writing, storytelling, or hearsay; (5) *invective* and threat, exemplified in random and unpredictable violence to punish real or imagined crimes; (6) *omission,* and concealment of the process by a sort of paralepsis that claims discrimination to be self-evidently valid and natural" (x-xi).

This schema, operating at all levels of language from the simplest on, enforces the systematic repression of the black portion of the unconscious, of the memory, and therefore of the story. This whole process is, for Snead, the force which pressures Quentin to repeat the story of Sutpen exactly as it is told to him, a story which fails to make sense because its coherence has been ravaged by the psychological schism within the culture itself, because half of its major players have been withheld in the repression of the black. It is Shreve who uncovers the truth, who through his critical questioning of the story restores the missing characters and actions and thus the story's meaning (125-131).

Charting the important places in *Absalom* reveals a careful cross-section of the history of North America since Columbus. Quentin's Cambridge and Sutpen's Virginia Tidewater: North and South at their very inception, the first footholds of each on the continent, the one founded for God, the other for profit, where the first decisions regarding slavery were made. These are the English-speaking colonies which revolted against England and drove ruthlessly westward across the middle third of the continent, which, as the United States, decimated their aboriginal neighbors, and agonized over the problem of slavery. Sutpen's West Virginia symbolizes An American paradox, a state which revolted against its own capital in Virginia and was born during the Civil War, a state which neither kept many slaves nor outlawed slavery, a state which is integral to the Northern industrial network, which is culturally oriented toward the South, yet which belongs to neither North nor South.

This section of the continent was not alone in its experience with slavery; Haiti and Bon's New Orleans represent the French experience with an even crueler version of the same economic system as that in the Southern states. New Orleans is a product of Canadian history, having been settled by French-speaking people who were driven from New Brunswick by the British in the Eighteenth Century. Spain is implied only in small but significant errors: Sutpen believed Eulalia Bon to have been "Spanish" (355), and Shreve confuses Haiti with its neighboring island, treating them as a combined location, "Porto Rico or Haiti or wherever it was" (298).

Shreve comes from Edmonton, Alberta, the continent's northernmost metropolis, which grew within the jurisdiction of the Hudson's Bay Company, which governed the Far North from 1670 on. This section has a history virtually unique in the experience of European North America. Unlike the United States and the southern French colonies, the region never imported slaves from Africa. Unlike the Spanish colonies and later on the United States, the Hudson's Bay Company never exploited or dispossessed the aboriginal tribes within its territories, but from the beginning pursued a trade policy which was beneficial to both sides, exchanging guns, tools, and cooking utensils for furs (Newman 192- 229), and thus supplying the natives with implements which enhanced their standard of living and strengthened their culture. In this region, the natives enjoyed a continuing rapport with their ancestral lands, and equal protection under British law. Finally, unlike the other English-speaking areas in the U.S. and Canada, this region never sought to dominate the French- and Spanish-speaking territories on the continent. The Hudson's Bay Territories occupied an area larger than most of the world's empires, and yet escaped the record of injustice which has tormented the rest of the continent.

Henry Sutpen's ability to accept the fact of incest but not miscegenation between Charles and Judith marks out a boundary in the evolution of human consciousness in terms of its increasing ability to bear the burden of guilt, as schematized by Brown: "The man who gives seeks to get rid of his guilt by sharing it. The man who takes is strong enough to shoulder his own burden of guilt. Christian man is strong enough to recognize that the debt is so great that only God can redeem it. Modern secular Faustian man is strong enough to live with irredeemable damnation." (LD 280). Those who founded Harvard College, like Goodhue Coldfield, lived in hope of God's redemption; Thomas Sutpen is overtly a type of Faust, and Henry, arriving at the Faustian or Romantic consciousness, shares with Quentin the ability to accept eternal damnation as a consequence of transgressing the incest taboo, which originated in the archaic mind and has universally governed the structure of family and religion ever since. Both Henry and Quentin arrive at the consciousness of Byron and Shelley, yet neither can accept the fact of living on a continent built upon the blood of men of another color. This burden of guilt is too great for the Faustian Ego; its transcendence, which necessarily involves *the merging of colors,* is the project of Brown's envisioned higher stage of evolution, *Dionysian Man.* Both Henry and Quentin arrive at the frontier of Dionysian consciousness, only to find death at its threshold.

The figure of Dionysus is the goal of our strange quest, for it is a figure uniting Nature with the Unconscious, and restoring both of these influences, which have been ravaged and buried by the ascendancy of rationalism and commerce. Dionysian man is man no longer alienated from himself, man healed and made whole again. This is the man who first emerged as a major force only in the 1960's, when the racial barriers which have divided us for such a long time finally began to crumble, and when America at last began to confront the basic prejudices it held from the beginning. Dionysian man arrives too late to help Quentin Compson, and many of those in today's South who are descended from his generation still resist the advance of the Dionysian Ego.

Thomas Sutpen

The external world itself is nothing but the projections of psychology. What was within returns from without . . . such occultism . . once coded as knowledge . . determines the social conditionality in which it may be decoded. If *The Cantos* is 'the tale of the tribe', then it equally well seeks to construct the tribe whose tale it is telling: the subject who succeeds in reading the poem is posited as a member of the imaginary tribe whose ideology structures the tale. . . . The animistic tribe is literalized in the mythic *Volk,* organized around the all-powerful figure of the Leader and the racially based gods and demons, in pursuit of the total implementation of tribal destiny.

> Martin A. Kayman,
> *The Modernism*
> *of Ezra Pound* 156-57

Primitive man does not analyze and does not work out why another man is superior to him. If another is cleverer and stronger than he, then he has mana, he is possessed of a stronger power... Historically the mana-personality evolves into the hero and the godlike being, whose earthly form is the priest. How very much the doctor is still mana is the whole plaint of the analyst!

> Carl Jung, "The Relations
> Between the Ego and the
> Unconscious" *245.*

The shaman is far enough from us so that we can recognize that he is, to put it mildly, a little mad; and, as we have seen, psychoanalysis discerns an intrinsic insanity in sublimation. "Pure intelligence," says Ferenczi, "is in principle madness."

> Norman O. Brown, "Apollo
> and Dionysus" in LD 158.

1.

Thomas Sutpen, the superior man, the tyrant, commands man and matter, ordering these into the Design, an abstract concept, by which he masters the tribe, the community, exerting an influence beyond his own time. Design and Power: Apollonian structures which cannot be held in stasis indefinitely -- they must yield to more dynamic forces or crumble into the dust of oblivion. We consider, then the rise and fall of Thomas Sutpen, historical figure within the fictive field of *Absalom, Absalom!*

2.

The psychoanalytical inquiry into the historical figure, the tyrant, follows two avenues, the first designated by the question, "what are the unconscious forces that underlie the individual who make up the collective, the tribe, Nation, or Community, to which the Tyrant, the Caesar or Napoleon or President of the United States, appeals?" This question can be reformulated thus: "what is it about the Tyrant that appeals to the individual psyche, thus enabling him to weld many individuals into a Collective, a Following?"

The second question is designated by the issue of the personality of the Tyrant. What unconscious forces motivate him? What are the features of the structure of sublimation which manifests itself as a Will to Power, propelling him into the implementation of a Design? These are the issues we must bring to bear on the career of Thomas Sutpen.

3.

For Sutpen, slavery is the domination of primitive men. His are not the outwardly gentle and conscious negroes that were bought and sold in the slave-markets of the South. The slaves he brings into Yoknapatawpha are the same kind, possibly the same ones, as he subdues in Haiti during the rebellion. These are men who practice magic, "a pig's bone with a little rotten flesh still clinging to it, a few chicken feathers, a stained dirty rag with a few pebbles tied up in it found on the old man's pillow one morning" (252); they instill terror by manipulating the corpse of a house servant, and create a "throbbing and trembling with the drums and chanting" (253). There is no abstract or Apollonian way to govern such men; they would fail to understand let alone respect a bill of indenture, and shooting at them is to shoot "at no enemy but at the Haitian night itself" (253). The revolt is the image of the Dionysian: the night, the drums, the fire, "the blank wall of black secret faces" (252), each undifferentiated, carrying out without thinking the will of "the little island" which is "the halfway point between what we call the jungle and what we call civilization" (250), its "soil manured with black blood from two hundred years of oppression and exploitation" (251).

4.

How Sutpen subdues the rebels is not told. But these are probably the same men as he brings to Yoknapatawpha in 1833, animal-like men whom Sutpen uses in hunting 'to drive the swamp like a pack of hounds" (36), and whom "the coon-hunter Akers claimed to have waked one of them out of the absolute mud like a sleeping alligator" (36). They are undifferentiated from nature; they appear to lack consciousness altogether. These are the laborers who build the Sutpen mansion: "while the negroes were working Sutpen never raised his voice at them, that instead he led them, caught them at the psychological instant by example, by some ascendency of forbearance rather than by brute fear" (37). But Sutpen's psychological superiority is ultimately based on his physical superiority, as the fights indicate. Rosa describes these: "in the center two of his wild negroes fighting, naked, fighting not as white men fight, with rules and weapons, but as negroes fight, to hurt one another quick and bad" (29). Here the distinction is present between fighting as a sublime, cerebral act, (perhaps involving an abstraction; honor perhaps) and fighting as a physical, primal event, in which Sutpen himself participates,

> naked to the waist and gouging at one another's eyes as if they should not only have been the same color, but should have been covered with fur too. Yes, it seems that on certain occasions, perhaps at the end of the evening, the spectacle, as a grand finale or perhaps as a matter of sheer deadly forethought toward the retention of

supremacy, domination, he would enter the ring with one of the negroes himself (29).

He masters his slaves as he masters nature, by meeting them on their own ground, by accomplishing the Dionysian descent, risking the loss of his own individuation, fighting with them on their own terms, working with them day after day, "all stark naked...plastered over with mud against the mosquitoes, distinguishable from one another by his beard and eyes alone" (37).

5.

Sutpen's Dionysian contact with the primal, the naked and therefore unrepressed, is at the same time the foundation of the Apollonian image by which he masters his white neighbors, who journey out from town to watch the house "rise, carried plank by plank and brick by brick out of the swamp" (37), and spread tales of his strange project; these men later on become spectators at the fights.

6.

Sutpen *implicates* the townsmen in his enterprise by the payment of a gold coin to the County Recorder. This action points to the unconscious process by which "man gives to get rid of the burden of guilt. Of course it does not get rid of guilt . . . but it does represent man's first attempt at a solution. Guilt is mitigated by being shared; man entered social organization in order to share guilt" (Brown, "Filthy Lucre", 268-69).

He has taken, probably stolen, a hundred square miles of land from Ikkemotubbe, and he is able to keep them even though he immediately leaves the region, by the *registration* of the *deed*. The *"virgin bottom land"* (34, emphasis mine) is transformed into a surveyed abstraction within the context of the larger abstractions of *county* and *state,* sets of written laws centering around august, temple-like structures, the *courthouse* and the *capitol.* The "virgin bottom land" becomes "Sutpen's Hundred" because the collective accepts it as such; this illusion is powerful enough to allow Sutpen to retain the *estate* because the society is secure enough to defend the illusions by which it exists. Sutpen seals the transaction which enables him to join the society by the giving of the symbol of excrement, of concentrated wealth, the gold coin.

7.

Sublimation . . . rests on the mind-body dualism . . . its goal is the elevation of spirit above matter (Brown, "Apollo and Dionysus" 157).

The psychoanalytical theory of infantile sexuality and its sublimation insists that there is a hidden connection between higher spiritual activity and the lower organs of the body (LD 203).

The house, then, is virtually a metaphor for the sublimation process, being raised by naked men literally out of the excremental mud, and worked into an abstract design provided by the French architect. The house is a "dream of grim and castlelike magnificence," (38) "the largest edifice in the county, not excepting the courthouse itself," (39) amid a complex of formal gardens "almost as large as Jefferson itself at the time" (38).

The Design goes through a strange interim stage lasting three years, during which the house stands "unpainted and unfurnished, without a pane of glass or a doorknob or hinge in it, . . wild turkey ranged within a mile of the house and deer came light and colored like smoke and left delicate prints in the formal beds where there would be no flowers for four years yet" (39). The house is more the palace of Dionysus than Apollo: it is not clearly distinguished from nature. It is the scene of drinking-and-hunting parties involving the wild negroes who hunt as animals hunt, and fights among the same. He treats his neighbors, the audience, voyeurs, viewers of the Primal Scene, to the spectacle of the Dionysian.

8.

Sutpen is ever careful to give more than he accepts in return. At the time of his arrival in Jefferson he declines to drink with anyone because "he did not have the money with which to pay his share or return the courtesy" (34), but later, when the house is built and he begins to entertain the hunting parties, this changes: "he drank very sparingly save when he himself had managed to supply some of the liquor. His guests would bring whiskey out with them but he drank of this with a sort of sparing calculation as though keeping mentally . . . a sort of spiritual solvency between the amount of whiskey he accepted and the amount of running meat which he supplied to the guns" (40). Thus he is able to hold his neighbors in a state of obligation: "prestige and power are conferred by the ability to give" ("Filthy Lucre" 264).

9.

The furnishing of the mansion and the wedding of Sutpen and Ellen Coldfield happen at the same time, more than coincidentally. Sutpen had refused General Compson's offer to loan him the money with which to buy the furnishings, because he "did not need to borrow money . . . because he intended to marry it" (41). This transaction equates the genital act with money; the dowry taking precedence over the living body of the bride. On the unconscious level the dowry money is given in exchange for the phallus of the groom. The economic nature of the marriage is broader than this, however: Sutpen enters the Methodist church "to find a wife exactly as he would have gone to the Memphis market to buy livestock or slaves" (42).

Living beings, even human beings are reduced to a monetary value; erotic impulses are displaced by the symbol of unnourishing filth; Sutpen's choice of a bride is an *investment*. The bride's father is perhaps the only "guiltless" man in the county, "a Methodist steward, a merchant.. .a man with a name for absolute and undeviating and even Puritan uprightness in a country and time of lawless opportunity, who neither drank nor gambled nor even hunted" (43). Goodhue Coldfield is a thoroughly Apollonian man, who in his incapacity to bear guilt, observes the limit. Sutpen attempts through his marriage to involve the town in "whatever felony which produced the mahogany and crystal, he was forcing the town to compound it" (43). The townspeople believe the sublime furnishings of the mansion to originate in filth and crime 'performed in the lurking dark of a muddy landing and with a knife from behind" (44). Sutpen allows himself to be arrested, no longer naked and muddy but impeccably dressed and bearing a genteel manner, being followed by a large crowd to the courthouse, again risking the descent into the collective, this time in the archetype of the Scapegoat. The bond for his release is signed by Compson and Coldfield; he implicates those whom the people dare not impugn.

10.

Life Against Death cited:

> Privilege is prestige, and prestige, in its fundamental nature as in the etymology of the word, means deception and enchantment. Again the line of development is continuous from the magician-leader of the simpler societies to the priest-king or god-king of the first civilizations, as indeed Frazer showed fifty years ago. Power was originally sacred, and it remains so in the modern world. Again we must not be misled by the flat antimony of the sacred and the secular, and interpret "secularization" what is only a metamorphosis of the sacred. If there is a class which has nothing to lose but its chains, the chains that bind it are self-imposed, sacred obligations which appear as objective realities with all the force of a neurotic delusion (252).

> It has long been known that the first markets were sacred markets, the first banks were temples, the first to issue money were priests or priest-kings (246).

> From the standpoint of the original protestant theology, the deification of capitalism and of the calling is the deification of the Devil, or at least an utter confusion between God and the Devil. From the psychoanalytical point of view, if the Devil is Death, and capitalism is the Devil, then modern Protestantism's alliance with capitalism means its complete surrender to the death instinct (224).

> And since the Devil is lord of this world, we may say, in psychoanalytical terms, that Luther sees civilization as having an essentially anal-sadistic structure, as essentially constructed by the sublimation of anality (225-26).

And Mr. Compson:

> Mr. Coldfield apparently intended to use the church into which
> he had invested a certain amount of sacrifice and doubtless self-
> denial and certainly actual labor and money for the sake of what
> might be called a demand balance of spiritual solvency, exactly as
> he would have used a cotton gin in which he considered himself
> to have incurred either interest or responsibility, for the ginning of
> any cotton which he or any member of his family, by blood or by
> marriage had raised -- that, and no more (49-50).

Cotton, the cash crop which drives the Mississippi economy, the
material basis of Sutpen's wealth.

11.

Coldfield desires a small wedding, Sutpen a large one: "not the
anonymous wife and the anonymous children, but the two names, the
stainless wife and the unimpeachable father-in-law, on the license, the
patent. Yes, patent, with a gold seal and red ribbons too if that had
been practicable" (51).

Mr. Compson attributes to women in general and thereby to Ellen
the desire for 'the image of themselves walking to music and turning
heads, in all the symbolical trappings and circumstances of ceremonial
surrender of that which they no longer possess . . . and why not, since
to them the actual and authentic surrender can only be (and has been)
a ceremony like the breaking of a banknote to buy a ticket for the train
(49).

The desire for the ritual is erotically based: for Sutpen, anally, or
anti-anally, and for Ellen, genitally.

12.

Sutpen's relationship to the community is expressed in oral
imagery:

> that public opinion which at some moment during the five
> preceding years had swallowed him even though he had never lain quiet

on its stomach, had performed one of mankind's natural and violent and inexplicable voltefaces and regurgitated him. And it did not help him any that at least two of the teeth in the outraged jaw served instead as props to hold the jaw open and impotent while he walked out of it unharmed" *(52)*.

Though the aunt tries to thrust Sutpen and the wedding "down the town's throat," (54), it is not the townspeople who attend the wedding, which takes place at night by torchlight, like a Dionysian revel. The guests come from "beneath [the town]," from the livery stable and the drover's tavern *(54)*, not the respectable but the disreputable. After the ceremony, these guests bombard the groom with dirt and debris and refuse *(56-57)*, careful not to hit the bride. Sutpen's mouth, until now completely hidden by his beard, suddenly becomes visible.

13.

Nevertheless, the Sutpens are able to raise more cotton than anyone else; their plantation, as large as the town and centered about the mansion just as the town centers on the courthouse, becomes the most prosperous in the county. Sutpen is "feared" by his neighbors who believe that "the plantation was just a blind to his actual dark avocation" or that "he had found some way to juggle the cotton market itself and so get more per bale than honest men could" or "that the wild niggers . . . had the power to actually conjure more cotton per acre than any tame ones had ever done" (72). At any rate, "he was accepted; he obviously had too much money now to be rejected" (72). He even hires the sheriff who once arrested him to work as his overseer (72).

14.

This stage of our inquiry seeks to examine the unconscious motives of Sutpen himself, the elements of his background which impel his formulation and execution of the Design. Much of the material for this is provided in Chapter VII, which is a retelling of a retelling; that is, Quentin tells Shreve at Harvard what Sutpen himself told General Compson in the woods as the wild Negroes hounded the runaway French architect who was directing the building of the mansion.

15.

Sutpen's native West Virginia (neither North nor South nor yet divided from the Old Dominion) is a Dionysian milieu: "the land belonged to anybody and everybody and so the man who would go to the trouble and work to fence off a piece of it and say 'This is mine' was crazy; and as for objects, nobody had any more of them than you did because everybody had just what he was strong enough or energetic enough to take and keep, and only that crazy man would go to the trouble to take or even want more than what he could eat or swap for powder and whiskey" (221). In West Virginia, life revolves around what is concrete and basic: sustenance, war as pure physical encounter, and whiskey, the hard essence of the barleycorn distilled in a hard land, the intoxicant, the gift of Dionysus.

16.

The displacement of the libido from the body outward into objects; the process of wealth. Wealth; a detachment, as splitting, a dissociation of the body; a form of madness. Wealth in terms of objects is seen as "crazy" by the West Virginians, who calculate worth "by lifting anvils or gouging eyes or how much whiskey you could drink then get up and walk out of the room" (226). They are like the warrior caste Nietzsche describes in *The Genealogy of Morals,* valuing "combat, adventure, the chase, the dance, war games, etc." (167), incapable of sustained hatred because they redress all wrongs spontaneously and violently; they do not seek revenge through reasoning calculation.

The mountain country is opposed to the Virginia Tidewater, "a country all divided and fixed and neat with people living on it all divided and fixed and neat because of what color their skins happened to be and what they happened to own, and where a certain few men not only had the power over life and death and barter and sale over others, but they had living human men to perform the endless repetitive personal offices, such as pouring the very whiskey from the jug and putting the glass into a man's hand or pulling off his boots for him to go to bed, that all men have had to do for themselves since time began and would have to do until they died but which no man that [Sutpen] knew of

27

had ever thought of evading any more than he had thought of evading the effort of chewing and swallowing and breathing" (221-22). In the mountains this place exists in the form of "vague and cloudy tales of Tidewater splendor" (222); there it is a distant dream, whereas in its own place it is the dream in common, a dream that structures a society. It is the demesne of Apollo.

17.

The journey, "the fall" (222), of Sutpen's family into the Tidewater coincides with the death of his mother: "He said something to Grandfather about his mother dying about that time and how his pap said she was a fine wearying woman and that he would miss her; and something about how it was the wife that had got, his father even that far West" (223).

The "mountain cove" (225) as regressive fantasy, "where they had all been born." The family is large, the mother must have been continually pregnant; the presence of an infant in the journey suggests that that mother died during childbirth. The journey itself is regressive, moving not westward where independence is available for the taking of its responsibility, where the old metaphor of life as the daily course of the sun would dictate, but rather back to the old country on the seaboard, the Mother Country. It represents "some easy place or time, some escape from the hardship of getting food and keeping warm the mountain way"; Sutpen speculates that his father went there 'not for the promised job but for the ease, having faith perhaps in the blood kinship to evade the labor" (223).

The regressive journey, the return to the Golden Age, to Eden, the security of infancy.

18.

...and by this time a huge bull of a nigger, the first black man, slave, they had ever seen, who emerged with the old man over his shoulder like a sack of meal and his -- the nigger's -- mouth loud with laughing and full of teeth like tombstones (AA 225).

The Negro associated with death, with the devouring earth. To the children he is monstrous, "a huge bull," the Minotaur, having the ability to devour the father, "a sack of meal." The negro is an appearance, a "balloon face" (232), which when beaten is "no actual nigger, living creature, living flesh to feel pain and writhe and cry out" (232); he has nothing to do with the anger of Sutpen's father; he is only a projection, a target, just as he is the Doorman, the representative of the Man in the Big House, Pettibone (small penis), "Hell fire, that goddam son of a bitch Pettibone's nigger" (231), the negro in the tavern, the negro who turns him from the door (232-33).

Sutpen repeats the beating of the owner's Negroes in Haiti, during the uprising, and in the barn at Sutpen's Hundred, here employing other Negroes to do the beating for him, just as Pettibone employed negroes to remove his shoes. The fight against the negro is the fight against death, which in Haiti Sutpen nearly loses.

19.

The mountain cabin; "boiling with children like the one he was born in -- men and grown boys who hunted or lay before the fire on the floor while the women and older girls stepped back and forth across them to reach the fire to cook" (221): a stage and an audience for the primal scene, the parents in coitus, the scene which repeats itself with every pregnancy of the mother, the sister, echoed in the fantastic life of the spectator, the child, Sutpen. The cabin: life polymorphous, bonded body to body, the taboo of incest transcended, the family structure: anarchy.

This scene over and against the plantation, Sutpen's Hundred, with its strict organization of patriarchy, Mother, Father, Sister, Brother, the prohibition of incest, the segregation into gender and generation, the segregation into black and white.

20.

The exodus is an initiation; the wandering is a rite of passage, from Troy to new Troy, from England to New England. From the mother to the mother; we are getting nowhere. And the wandering is all in the mother: the churinga [for Sutpen, the classroom information on the West Indies, the gold Spanish coin] which the initiate takes with him on his way, marked with the concentric maze pattern, symbolizes and magically achieves the unity of the infant with the mother ("Nature" in LD 41).

The house, itself a symbol of the mother: Sutpen's Hundred, landscape house and labyrinthine gardens, built and decorated for the sake of the wife, the mother Ellen; the Haitian mansion, in which Sutpen crouches in the hot darkness, wielding the phallic musket, attended and afterwards nursed by the planter's daughter.

Sutpen is the voyeur, the spectator in relation to the Tidewater Planter, stealing away from home to gaze idly at the man in the hammock, drinking, barefoot and attended by the negro (228). His rejection at the door of the Tidewater mansion by the "monkey nigger" (232), representing father and phallus, is a reenactment of the Primal Scene in which the child is driven away from the mother, into whom he desires entry. This moment is the moment of castration, when the child, frozen with fear and excitement, becomes the spectator, and the soul divorced from the body.

21.

The insult is incomprehensible to Sutpen, because, as Quentin rightly intuits, of his origin in the polymorphous environment of the mountain cabin, in the family as "passel" (223), a den of hibernating snakes, thousands tangled into a single body. Here the Combined Object, the parents in coitus, is no cause for consternation, being expanded to include brothers, sisters, all members of the family, in a single polymorphous Object.

Part of the insulted child remains inside the womb, symbolically, in a career which is a vicarious enactment of the Primal Scene. This is the child as Penis, the soul detached from the body. Sutpen responds to the insult by flight, by retreating into his secret place: "He said he crawled back into the cave and sat with his back against the uptorn roots, and thought" (223). He is Urizen retreating into himself, reasoning, sublimating. His reasoning continues in an unbroken monologue through that day and the day in 1864, in General Compson's office; he tries to comprehend the collapse of his design; he cannot "get it straight" (223); he cannot find where he made "the mistake in it" (263), for the root of the problem lies in the unconscious, repressed, and reason is an evasion, a flight from life, something other than the real problem.

22.

Sutpen, in short, is prevented by his innocence from learning anything about the actual concrete relations that operate in a complex society, or in a family that belongs to such a society. All he can take in to shape a morality and a conscience with is an abstract and therefore static 'design' -- the word is well chosen -- which then defines his character and identity. It is a monomania which enables him to become (twice) a rich plantation owner, the very pattern (in a sharply ironic sense) of the aristocrat, but which will never let him become a man, with human feelings, human virtues, and a human capability for the continual compromises imposed by human inconsistency, weakness, and error. Because he is unwilling or unable to bend, his doom in Faulkner's dynamic world is to be broken by the ubiquitous winds and floods of change (Adams 190).

The Plantation, (surveyed, square and registered) is not the Land (hill, forest and stream), and the demise of Thomas Sutpen is the crucial point in the conflict between Apollo, the god of the image (design), of stasis; the eternal sculpture, division and dream, and Dionysus, god of movement, change, the dance, the bringing together of all things, the conflict between intellect and the fluid forces of nature. Thomas Sutpen is destroyed by the very forces which, when allied with, brought him to wealth and influence. As Adams has perceived, the chain of events which leads to Sutpen's death is equal to his systematic denial and insulting of the Dionysian forces which throughout his life have aided him.

23.

If normal adult sexuality is a pattern which has grown out of the infantile delight in the pleasurable activity of all parts of the human body, then what was originally a much wider range, concentrated on one particular (the genital) organ, and subordinated to an aim derived not from the pleasure-principle but from the reality-principle, namely, propagation (in Freudian terminology, the genital function) ("Sexuality and Childhood" in LD 26-27).

'On this night I am speaking of (and until my first marriage, I might add) I was still a virgin. You will probably not believe that, and if I were to try to explain it you would disbelieve me more that ever. So I will only say that that too was a part of the design which I had in my mind' (Voice of Thomas Sutpen in AA 248).

In the above citation, Sutpen speaks of the time of the Haitian rebellion, when he was twenty years old, the time during which he won the hand-in-marriage of the planter's daughter. This pattern, already established, constitutes the course of Sutpen's sexual expression throughout his life; he copulates only in order to beget children, and otherwise devotes his energy to other projects, equally subordinate to the reality principle. The dilemma he faces in his last days is expressed in the symbolism of the ejaculating phallus: *"When he realized that there was more in his problem than just lack of time, that the problem contained some superdistillation of this lack: that he was now past sixty and that possibly he could get but one more son, had at best but one more son in his loins, as the old cannon might know when it has just one more shot in its corporeality"* (279).

24.

Sutpen, the invincible demon, unconsciously creates his own demise via his actions following his return from the war. At each phase of the sequence of events, he has the option of saving himself wasted effort, of enjoying what he has and accepting the aid of those who come to him, and at each crisis, he rejects this option, and multiplies rather than merely adds to his difficulties with the rejection of each potential ally.

Returning from the war, he need not restore his lands to what they once were in order to make them productive enough to sustain himself in comfort; nevertheless, he initiates the attempt to do so, even while making enemies of John Sartoris and his followers, who offer friendship within the context of a new social order in which Sutpen could enjoy his former position of privilege and status.

Had Sutpen acknowledged Charles Bon as even an illegitimate son, he might have not only retained his heir apparent, Henry, but would have had the help of his two able-bodied and intelligent sons. Or he might have accepted a matriarchal line of succession, either by passing the land to Judith, or by marrying Rosa and accepting the possibility of a female offspring, of by accepting the daughter of Milly Jones, which would have spared him the death he died.

It is easy to see the presence of genital sexuality at the root of each of these events. Sutpen wishes to *engender* the land himself, without the aid of his neighbors; his sexuality is an attempt to engender a *dynasty*, an attempt to impose his Design on the future. Charles Bon, the firstborn son, unacceptable because of an artificial distinction between black and white, (a distinction, as we have seen, rooted in the fear of death), the rejected son and potential ally, works against the father by attempting to *marry* the daughter, and alienates the heir (Henry) from the father. And Rosa Coldfield is outraged by Sutpen's proposal, *"luckily . . . just a spotting shot with a light charge, and the old gun, the old barrel and carriage none the worse; only next time there might not be enough powder for both a spotting shot and a full-sized load . . . "* (279). And finally, Milly Jones, "started . . . like you start a rabbit out of a brier patch, with a little chunk of dried mud thrown by hand" (281), like the American Indian seduced with candy and cheap trade goods, won with the sublime gift of anality where paternal authority is no longer legal tender.

In observing the span of Thomas Sutpen's life, it is possible to trace, as we have here, a logic of the Death Instinct at work behind the motions of sexuality.

25.

Civilized man asserts his individuality, and makes history. But the individuality he asserts is not life-affirming or life-enjoying, but the life-negating (ascetic) individuality of (Faustian) discontent and guilt. Civilized individuality, in Nietzsche's image, does not want itself, but wants children, wants heirs, wants an estate. Life remains a war against death-civilized man, no more than archaic man, is not strong enough to die -- and death is overcome by accumulating time- defying monuments. These accumulations of stone and gold make possible the discovery of the immortal soul. . . . But the inevitable irony redresses the balance in favor of death. Death is overcome on condition that the real actuality of life passes into these immortal and dead things; money is the man; the immortality of an estate or a corporation resides in the dead things which alone endure. By the law of the slow return of the repressed, the last stage of history is, as Luther said, the dominion of death in life; the last stage of the polis is, as Mumford said, Nekropolis ("Filthy Lucre" in LD 286).

Indeed, Sutpen is portrayed as a kind of Faust, whose grand design represents the rational ego's will to power in its attempt to do away with the undesigned and irrational (Irwin 84).

26.

When Sutpen was a child, he received an affront from the black servant of a rich plantation owner. He was told that he could not come to the front door of the planter's house, he had to go around to the back because he was white trash, because he and his family were not as good as the plantation owner. ...Accepting this ideal of patriarchal power, Sutpen determines his fate -- henceforth, he will no longer receive the affront, he will deliver it. Thus, he rejects his first wife and son because they are not good enough to share the position to which he aspires. And he passes that fated repetition on to his sons -- to Charles Bon, who returns thirty years later seeking admittance to the rich plantation owner's "house" (and thereby represents the return of the repressed traumatic affront of Sutpen's boyhood) and to Henry, who, acting as his father's surrogate, delivers the final affront to Bon, killing him at the gates of the house to prevent his entering" (Irwin 97-99).

The repetition-compulsion, like civilization, serving the Death Instinct. In order to culminate in Sutpen's death, the parallel must remain unconscious, the returning repressed must pass the Censor. It is not Charles Bon, who danced, drank, and slept in the mansion at Sutpen's Hundred, who plays the part of the final child at the door, but rather Wash Jones, who, like young Sutpen, is scorned even by the planter's slaves, "still carrying fish and animals he killed (or maybe stole) and vegetables up to the house when that was about all Mrs. Sutpen and Judith (and Clytie too) had to live on, and Clytie would not let him come into the kitchen with the basket even, saying, 'stop right there, white man. Stop right where you is. You aint never crossed this door while Colonel was here and you aint going to cross it now" (281). Jones, then, stands in relation to Thomas Sutpen as Sutpen stands in relation to the Tidewater planter, and when Sutpen comes for the last time to Jones' cabin, the two men stand in relation to each other as Henry and Bon stand to each other at the gate of Sutpen's Hundred.

'Stand back, Wash. Don't you touch me .
'I'm going to tech you, Kernel' (286).

Don't you pass the shadow of this post, this branch, Charles;
and I am going to pass it, Henry (133).

In each case, the suitor standing at the gate, intimate with the daughter within, but cut down by the man of the house before he can reach her.

27.

Sutpen, having arrived at the occupation of Goodhue Coldfield, *'the ancient varicose and despairing Faustus fling his final main now with the Creditors hand already on his shoulder, running his little country store now for his bread and meat, haggling tediously over nickels and dimes with rapacious and poverty-stricken whites and negroes, who at one time could have galloped for ten miles in any direction without crossing his own boundary.*" (182), rendering payment unto the Creditor, atoning for his burden of guilt, expiation, himself the sacrifice, himself the scapegoat. The land itself had been his body and his being extended to the corners of the Hundred; now, an old man, facing the old man with the scythe, Father Time, the Grim Reaper, cutting down the Kernel, John Barleycorn, the Grape, pressed, the Lamb, slaughtered.

28.

An old legend has it that King Midas hunted a long time in the woods for the wise Silenus, companion of Dionysus, without being able to catch him. And when he had finally caught him the king asked him what he considered man's greatest good. The daemon remained sullen and uncommunicative until finally, forced by the king, he broke into a shrill laugh and spoke: 'Ephemeral wretch, begotten by accident and toil, why do you force me to tell you what it would be your greatest boon not to hear? What would be best for you is quite beyond your reach: not to have been born, not to be. to be nothing. But the second best is to die soon (The Birth of Tragedy 29).

Wash Jones had viewed his friend and ally as a dream, a "proud galloping image . . galloping through avatars which marked the accumulation of years, time, to the fine climax where it galloped without weariness or progress, forever and forever immortal beneath the brandished saber and the shot-torn flags rushing down a sky in color like thunder" (288), trusting the man because he is "brave" (284), because he has Mana. And the insult plunges him into contradiction *(I kaint have heard what I know I heard)* (288), and formless chaos (Wash must not have felt the very earth under his feet) (288). Sitting alone, waiting calmly for nightfall, the mounted posse, and death, Jones knows the wisdom of Silenus: *"Brave! Better if narra one of them had ever rid back in '65' thinking Better if his kind and mine too had never drawn the breath of We on this earth. Better that all who remain of us be blasted from the face of it than that another Wash Jones should see his whole life shredded from him and shrivel away like a dried shuck thrown onto the fire . . . "* (290-91).

Apollo and Dionysus: the proud, rational, bright and beautiful Sutpen, the far-darter who rode many miles over land and sea and willed matter into form and Design, and Jones, who lives in the deep woods, brings food and aid to the Sutpens, who speaks in an ungrammatical and sometimes nonsensical voice, who offers his own granddaughter to the sustenance of life, yet who when scorned responds with bloody violence, the dissolution of whose ego compels the dissolution of his whole world, including the lives of his granddaughter and her baby, whom he continues to nourish until the final moments.

Apollo and Dionysus, friends drinking together beneath the scuppernong, partners in the shaping of a local culture, enemies tearing each other from this incarnation in the morning and evening of a single day.

The Extremes of Sublimation, Part I

New Orleans

In New Orleans, the river, the Dionysian place of "muddy landings" (44), and lawlessness and anonymous men moving outside the text of social hierarchy, the place of bottom thickets and fluidity and motion, which disregards the artificial boundaries of states by constantly changing its course, becomes the destination of boatloads of cotton, the marketplace of the entire valley, the gathering place of the cash crop of all plantations, all the Designs in all the counties upstream: an apocalypse: the City.

'The late city,' says Spengler, 'contradicts Nature in the lines of its silhouette, *denies* all Nature,' While 'the gigantic megalopolis the *city-as-world,* suffers nothing beside itself and sets about *annihilating* the country picture (Brown, "Filthy Lucre" in LD 282).

Mr. Compson envisions the country-bred Henry in the city, the City as a series of pictures which Charles Bon shows him, the city as *image,* as *illusion,* "exposing Henry slowly to the surface aspect -- the architecture a little femininely flamboyant and therefore to Henry opulent, sensuous, sinful: the inference of great and easy wealth measured by steamboat loads in place of a tedious inching of sweating human figures across cotton fields; the flash and glitter of carriage wheels, in which women, enthroned and immobile and passing rapidly across the vision, appeared like painted portraits beside man in linen a little finer and diamonds a little brighter and in broadcloth a little trimmer and with hats raked a little more above faces a little more darkly swaggering than any Henry had ever seen before" (120).

In the new space of the city, which is always a sacred space, man succeeds for the first time in constructing a new life which is wholly superfluous, and wholly sacred. A city is by definition divorced from primary food production, and therefore by definition superfluous; its whole economy is based on the economic surplus (LD 282).

And Henry,

> this grim humorless yokel out of a granite heritage where even
> the houses, let alone clothing and conduct, are built in the image
> of a jealous and sadistic Jehovah, put suddenly down in a place
> whose denizens had created their All-Powerful and His supporting
> hierarchy-chorus of beautiful saints and handsome angels in the
> image of their houses and personal ornaments and voluptuous lives
> (109).

Sutpen's Hundred is a small world marked off from the fields which
support it; New Orleans, with an immortal heaven built in its own
image, is a hierarchy of commerce, with many degrees of class, each
one more opulent and more *wasteful* than the last:

> the essence of sublimation is the reification of the superfluous-
> sacred in monumental, enduring form. Hence it is in the city that
> money finally settles upon the most durable precious metals. The
> city, in Gordon Childe's theory, presupposes metallurgy; but the
> metallurgy it presupposes is not metallurgy in the service of 'rational
> mastery over nature', or even in the service of war, but metallurgy
> in the service of conspicuous (and sacred) waste (LD 283).

Brown posits money as the basis of urban organization:

> Money is the heart of the new accumulation complex; the capacity
> of money to bear interest is its energy; its body is that fundamental
> institution of civilized man, the City (LD 281).

What Jefferson, with its courthouse and stones and streets and
churches achieves on a scale little larger than its surrounding plantations,
islands in the wilderness, New Orleans realizes in a scope which is
total. The City is an extreme of sublimation. "A city reflects the new
masculine aggressive psychology of revolt against the female principles
of dependence and nature" (LD 281-82).

At the extremes of sublimation, the Brunonian doctrine of opposites,
the idea of the *cirque politique* comes into play. If the Apollonian and
Dionysian are opposites in conflict, then the Apollonian development
of New Orleans should ultimately come to resemble the Dionysian.

This occurs in the city's institution by which the masculine *possesses* the feminine: the Octoroons. Bon describes them with "that pessimistic and sardonic cerebral pity of the intelligent for any human injustice of folly or suffering, "We -- the thousand, the white man -- made them, created and produced them; we even made the laws which declare that one eighth of a specified kind of blood shall outweigh seven eights of another kind" (115). He justifies this by invoking, inventing a cosmology consisting of the damned, the fieldhands and servants, and the elect who live in urban luxury, and a God Who approves of the men who "save" the octoroons, women who are

> taken at childhood, culled and chosen and raised more carefully that any white girl, any nun, than any blooded mare even . . . for . . . a price offered and accepted or declined through a system more formal than any that white girls are sold under since they are more valuable as commodities than white girls, raised and trained to fulfill a woman's sole end and purpose: to love, to be beautiful, to divert . . . chosen by some man who in return, not can and not will but *must*, supply her with the surroundings proper in which to love and be beautiful and divert, and who must usually risk his life or at least his blood for that privilege (117).

These women, the ultimate in superfluity, the ultimate in luxury, present a primal, Dionysian appearance: " -- a woman with a face like a tragic magnolia, the eternal female, the eternal Who-suffers" (114), the embodiment of "a female principle which existed, queenly and complete, in the hot equatorial groin of the world long before that white one of ours came down from the trees and lost its hair and bleached out -- a principle ... which her white sisters of a mushroom yesterday flee from in moral and outraged horror (116). For Henry, there are three classes of women, three arbitrary divisions based on sexuality, on the economic relationship with the male, and on racial distinction: "the virgins whom gentlemen someday married, the courtesans to whom they went while on sabbaticals to the cities, the slave girls and women upon whom the first caste rested and in certain cases to whom it doubtless owed the very fact of its virginity" (109). The Octoroon is a melding of all these categories: she is white and black, owned by a master, legally a slave, and at the same time opulent, a luxury, a courtesan, also a virgin, given over to a man in a morganatic ceremony, to be wife and mother to his child.

The ceremony is of African origin, performed by "a crone mumbling in a dungeon lighted by a handful of burning hair, something in a tongue which not even the girls themselves understood anymore"(l 17), something primitive, "rooted in nothing of economics for her or for any possible progeny since the very fact that we acquiesced, suffered the farce, was proof and assurance of that which the ceremony itself could never enforce"(l18). The Octoroon's child is no heir; it is something the men suffer, masochism, a humiliation inflicted by women.

Brown, in discussing the difficulty Freud experienced in developing a theory of aggression, posits the connection between Eros and the Death Instinct in the depths of the human psyche by identifying pleasure with the cessation of activity, with the repetition of the primal state preceding birth, a return to non-being which is Death. It is Death which gives a being its individuality, which the human is not strong enough to bear and therefore seeks to lose his identity in social organization ("Death, Time, and Eternity" in LD, Cf. Irwin 86-87).

Just as the repression of Life creates the City, the repression of Death creates aggression by deflecting the individual's inner instinct to die outward, onto others. Masochism is thus transformed into Sadism.

In New Orleans, the male allows the female to inflict humiliation on him; he in turn inflicts his pride, his *worthiness,* on his fellow male. Hence the form of dueling (doubling) which is inextricably linked with the keeping of the Octoroons, as Bon explains: "'the customary way is to stand back to back, the pistol in your right hand and the corner of the other cloak in your left. Then at the signal you begin to walk and when you feel the cloak taughten you turn and fire. Though there are some now and then, when the blood is especially hot or when it is still peasant blood, who prefer knives and one cloak." (113)

Anyone at all familiar with the custom of dueling in the Old South knows that that it is essentially show, a bluff, fought with poor pistols fired beyond the range of their accuracy. Thus the combatants could assuage their humiliation while at the same time minimizing the chance of someone actually getting hurt. But over the Octoroons the combatants fire at point blank range: the probability of one of them receiving a fatal wound is thus very high. The inevitability of such a contest in the career of an Octoroon-keeper means that accepting such chattel is to accept the certainty of one's own death, and for Brown, it is the Dionysian, unrepressed creature which freely accepts its own death. Thus, in New Orleans, the intensive accumulation of wealth makes it possible for one to *purchase* an experience which appears to be utterly Dionysian, yet which reflects the underlying structure of the Apollonian processes out of which it develops.

War

Now the slave emerges as a freeman; all the rigid, hostile walls which either necessity of despotism has erected between men are shattered. Now that the gospel of unity has sounded, each individual becomes not only reconciled to his fellow but actually at one with him -- as though the veil of Maya had been torn apart and there remained only shreds floating before the vision of mystical Oneness. Man now expresses himself through song and dance as the member of a higher community; he has forgotten how to walk, how to speak, and is on the brink of taking wing as he dances *(The Birth of Tragedy* 23).

The outbreak of the war in the spring of 1861 has the effect of canceling the usual roles and priorities of the people, drawing them "with food and bedding and servants, to bivouac among the families, the houses, of Oxford itself, to watch the gallant mimic marching and countermarching of the sons and the brothers, drawn all of them, rich and poor, aristocrat and redneck, by what is probably the most moving mass-sight of all human mass-experience" (122), the mustering and training of the Confederate army, an experience in a sense intensely Dionysian. The time of year, "April and May and June" (123), is the time when, according to Nietzsche, "Dionysiac stirrings arise through the powerful approach of spring, which penetrate with joy the whole frame of nature." (22) The Apollonian concepts of class and property are suspended, as is the concept of military rank: "private and colonel called each other by their given names as one man to another above the suave powdered shoulders of women, above the two raised glasses of scuppernong claret or bought champagne" (123). Equality among men, drinking, music and dancing by night "among the blazing candles" (122), by day the company drilling, being welded into a single will, preparing for war and death and deprivation but for now enjoying meals and love and comforts: these evoke a Dionysian mood, an atmosphere of unity and contradiction and brotherhood, arising spontaneously at the extremes of sublimation.

The scene is compared to "the spectacle of so many virgins going to be sacrificed to some heathen principle, some Priapus" (122), and the soldiers are preparing to fight and very possibly die for a principle designated "states' rights" just as their opponents fight for a principle designated "the Union", both abstractions constructed, as Sundquist shows (96-130), upon the unconscious fear and denial of the sexual amalgamation practiced on the Southern plantations, including Sutpen's Hundred. The war is based on the *denial* of the Dionysian effects of brotherhood and unity and equality. As Snead observes, "Faulkner does not err in depicting this extreme need for division as sexual in origin. The paradox that fuels Faulkner's major novels here emerges: the South's fear of racial mixing involves an element of undefined sexual desire for the denied other, and finally a fetishization of the other's tangibility" (105). This moment, on the eve of the war, conceals the Apollonian structure which underlies it: "the bright gallant deluded blood and flesh dressed in a martial glitter of brass and plumes . .the swing or crinoline," the "banded gold of rank, of an army even if not a war of gentlemen" (122-23); hence the equality of soldier and officer is based on the assumption of the same high social rank of both, based on the assumption of mutual worthiness of the pure white woman, again based of the unconscious fear and desire of miscegenation. Here is displayed all the extravagance of wealth that marks the sublimated society, emblematized by the "company's colors, the segments of silk cut and fitted but not sewn, from house to house until the sweetheart of each man in the company had taken a few stitches in it" (123). So much effort is expended in beautifying that which will become soiled and tattered and finally lost in the course of battle, though it is the very thing which structures the battle.

The effect of the war at Sutpen's Hundred is Dionysian in a less festive sense; that hardship that ensues in the wake of intense fighting, the absence of the landowners, the departure of the slaves, and the Union occupation of Mississippi demands a wastage of wealth, and demands labor in the service of life from those who until now had lived solely off the excess of wealth which they are now compelled to deplete. Mr. Compson describes Judith's participation in such labor:

> when she came to town now, in the made-over dress which all Southern women now wore, in the carriage still but drawn now by a mule, a plow mule, soon the plow mule, and no coachman to drive it either, to put the mule in the harness and take it out, to join the other women-there were wounded in Jefferson then-in the improvised hospital where *(the nurtured virgin, the supremely and traditionally idle)* they cleaned and dressed the *self-fouled bodies* of strange injured and dead and *made lint of the window curtains and sheets and linen on the houses* in which they had been born . . . *(125-26,* emphasis mine).

Excrement, both symbolic and literal, is no longer accumulated but disposed of, and the plantation and the labor of its owners are devoted almost entirely to the production of the family's own food: Judith, Clytie, and Wash Jones keep "a kitchen garden of sorts to keep them alive" (125) while the formal decorative gardens grow wild with weeds; the very idea of a weed is artificial, depending on the work of man and the negation of such, for nature does not distinguish between the weed and the useful plant.

The appearance of Wash Jones augments the Dionysian imagery of page 125:

> ...living in the abandoned fishing camp in the river bottom which Sutpen had built after the first woman -- Ellen -- entered his house and the last deer and bear hunter went out of it, where he now permitted Wash and his daughter and infant granddaughter to live, performing the heavy garden work and supplying Ellen and Judith and then Judith with fish and game now, who until Sutpen went away, had never approached nearer than the scuppernong arbor behind the kitchen where on Sunday afternoons he and Sutpen

would drink from the demijohn and the bucket of spring water which Wash fetched from almost a mile away.

The admission of Jones to the household consistent with the pattern of the breakdown of social distinctions; Wash himself is a Dionysian figure, a parallel to the mythic Dionysus, the vegetation god. Jones performs physical, as opposed to cerebral labor; he lives in the deep thicket on the river bottom, the flood-prone area of dense vegetation which coincides with the setting of much of *Go Down, Moses,* hunting and fishing, performing those cruel offices which are not distinguishable from kindness and nourishment, and especially serving as the bringer of the intoxicant to Sutpen, serving him beneath the vine of scuppernong, the only grape which grows well in the Deep South. The war itself can be interpreted as a metaphor for the conflict between Apollo and Dionysus, for here the two gods are closely ranged against one another, thus becoming nearly indistinguishable. Of all the novel's characters, Judith comes closest to achieving what Brown calls the Dionysian ego, that is, an ego which is strong enough to survive the breakup of the limits in relation to which individuation is accomplished. The description of Judith's Dionysian existence, which we have just discussed, is bracketed in the Faulknerian text by a description of Charles Bon being distinguished from his comrades, "removed to the isolation of commissioned rank," having "the slight and authorized advantage of saying *you* go there . . ." (124), and on page 126, allusions to Thomas Sutpen's commissioned rank, the deaths of Ellen and Goodhue Coldfield, and the Sutpen gravestones. The language of Dionysus bracketed by the monumental signs of Apollo, and the war is the stage on which this interplay is enacted.

Rosa Coldfield

To Rescue from Oblivion and to Perpetuate in the Memory of Future Generations the Heroic Patriotism of the Men of Leon County Who Died in the Civil War of 1861-1865 This Monument Is *Erected* By Their Country Women

> Obelisk, Lawn of Old Florida
> State Capitol, Tallahassee
> (emphasis mine)

Rosa Coldfield, of all the voices present or absent in the novel, is the one most deeply enmeshed in the fantastic. She speaks to Quentin out of a condition of Life-in-Death; who could dispute the application of the adjective "deathlike" in describing her existence. The metaphors Faulkner employs in describing her underline this implicitly. During "the long hot weary *dead* September afternoon," (7, emphasis mine) Rosa, wearing 'the eternal black" of mourning, speaks to Quentin in "the dim coffin-smelling room" (8); she is "one of the ghosts which had refused to lie still even longer than most had, telling him about old ghost times" (9). Her voice is described as "not ceasing but vanishing into and then out of the long intervals like a stream, a trickle running from patch to patch of dried sand" (8), an image of drought, of waters held back, of the waste land. The house itself is a figure of stagnation: "what Miss Coldfield still called the office because her father had called it that -- a dim hot airless room with the blinds all closed and fastened for forty-three summers because when she was a girl someone had believed that light and moving air carried heat and that dark was always cooler" (7). This room serves as a metaphor for a mind, closed off by the opinions of the past, through which air and light cannot carry out their cleansing and life-giving circulation; what is intended to be cool and comfortable ironically becomes hot and stifling. These are Faulkner's preliminary descriptions of a woman who composes "ode, eulogy, and epitaph" (11), a woman who, unlike her counterpart in Stevens' poem "Sunday Morning", gives her bounty to the dead.

Rosa measures her deathly life from the time when she broke her engagement to her brother-in-law Thomas Sutpen, shocked at Sutpen's proposition, his *"bald outrageous words exactly as if he were consulting with Jones or with some other man about a bitch dog or a cow or mare"* (168); a shock which leaves her "irrevocably husbanded to an abstract carcass of outrage and revenge" (180). She, metaphorically, like Faulkner's Emily Grierson literally, is married to a corpse, an abstraction, an Apollonian phantasm that displaces real life.

But prior to the commencement of these forty-three years, Rosa is already living within a world of strange fantasies, already obsessed with abstractions. Perhaps the most striking of these is the one concerning Charles Bon, whose death she likewise fails to accept, speaking of his corpse as *"the abstraction which we had nailed into a box,"* killed by *"a shot heard only by its echo"* (153). She cannot believe what she hasn't seen; she can't believe what she has not had the time and opportunity to reflect on and come to understand: *"It was too short, too fast, too quick; six hours of a summer afternoon saw it all -- a space too short to leave even the imprint of a body on a mattress, and blood can come from anywhere -- If there was blood, since I never saw him. For all I was allowed to know, we had no corpse; we even had no murderer (we did not even speak of Henry that day, not one of us . . ."* (152).

Rosa has neither the living nor the dead body of Charles Bon, only a web of fantasies surrounding him. Having repressed the fact of Henry's guilt, Rosa projects her subsequent anger onto Wash Jones, *"that brute who until Ellen died was not even permitted to approach the house from the front"* (134), who is closely connected with the reality of Bon's death, being responsible for carrying out the tasks the situation requires. He rides into Jefferson, calling out from the street, *"Air you Rosie Coldfield? Then you better come on out yon. Henry has done shot that durn French feller. Kilt him dead as beef"* (133). Jones articulates the reality of the fact in a way which allows no room for abstractions such as honor or reverence for the dead, abstractions which serve to repress the fact of death. Jones' statement is a naked rendering of the event, revealing to Rosa the materiality of what for her is a fantastic event, comparing the dead man to a dead steer, just as Rosa compares Sutpen's proposal for their mating to the mating of livestock. Jones' statement puns on an alternate meaning, in the exclamatory: "Air you, Rosie Coldfield!" This would be a command to open the windows, to abandon these fantasies which are robbing her of life, which would be the consequence of her accepting Jones' view of the event. What is interesting here is that Jones' exact words are recounted by Mr. Compson; Rosa herself makes no mention of them, even though her memory of the ride with Jones to Sutpen's Hundred is quite detailed and vivid, and she does remember the exact wording of several of his comments. We may assume, then, that Rosa represses this first graphic statement, which constitutes such a threat to her interior world. She subsequently transfers her affection for her dead fantasy lover, Bon, onto Thomas Sutpen's tombstone and thereby to Sutpen himself. The tombstone plays the same role in Rosa's fantastic life as the photograph of Bon on Judith's table during the summer of 1860. But we learn of Rosa's fascination with the stone from Mr. Compson also; Rosa herself omits this detail from her account of her sojourn to Sutpen's Hundred during 1865-66. It is also a detail which she represses, so that Sutpen's suggestion "that they breed together for test and sample" (177) represents a return of the repressed, which accounts for Rosa's shock and outrage more adequately than the given reason of trespass against puritan morality; Puritanism is an illusion than serves as a bulwark against the huge and monstrous world of the repressed. In fact, the text of Sutpen's exact statement comes from Shreve, and probably comes down from Mr. Compson via Quentin. Rosa herself promises to repeat these words to Quentin, understanding that she faces a choice between "[repeating] *the bold blank naked and outrageous words just as he spoke them, and bequeath you only the same aghast and outraged unbelief I knew when I comprehended what he meant; or take three thousand sentences and leave you with only that why? why? why? that that I have asked and listened to for almost fifty years*" (167). But she does not speak the words, rather something more like the three thousand sentences, using her words to conceal and repress what tried to break free in the original phrase.

So we find ourselves probing into the unbelievably complicated pathology of Rosa's ego, this life-in-death Waste Land which is her life. This last train of thought, which has proved strangely fruitful, creates the necessity for us to examine the unconscious associations clustering radiating from Wash Jones and his relation to Rosa's repression of Bon's death.

Jones and another man undertake the building of Bon's coffin, the sound of which Rosa has a profound aversion to:

I remember how during all that slow and sunny afternoon they hammered and sawed right under the parlor window- the slow, maddening rasp, rasp, rasp of the saw, the flat deliberate hammer blows that seemed as though each would be the last but was not, repeated and resumed just when the dulled attention of the wearied nerves, stretched beyond all resiliency, relaxed to silence and then had to scream again; until at last I went out there (and saw Judith in the barlot in a cloud of chickens, her apron cradled about the gathered eggs) and asked them why? why there? why must it be just there? and they both stopped long and more than long enough for Jones to turn and spit again and say, Because hit wouldn't be so fur to tote the box': and how before my very back was turned he -- one of them -- added further, out of some amazed and fumbling ratiocination of inertia, how 'Hit would be simpler yit to fetch him down and nail the planks around him, only maybe Missus Judy wouldn't like hit' (151).

In this passage, three things are apparent: Judith's calmness, her acceptance of the situation and her devotion to the needs of the living; the eggs *cradled* in her apron evoke nurturing, the world of the child and the mother who takes absolute care of it; Jones' unsentimental awareness of the reality of death; for Jones, as we have already seen, death is a very concrete matter, and his concerns here are strictly practical; so much weight is to be moved around; he has no abstract concerns about reverence; for him the casket is not a sacred vessel of the dead, but a box like any other box, and one that will not nourish him for bearing its weight [the word "box" itself is a vulgar term denoting the female genitalia and the coffin symbolizes the womb], and finally, Rosa's anguish and agitation; her mental state is carrying over into physical sensation, which becomes more apparent in her metaphorical treatment of her feelings toward the death: -- *I remember how as we carried him down the stairs and out to the waiting wagon I tried to take the full weight of the coffin to prove to myself that he was really in it. And I could not tell. I was one of the pallbearers, yet I could not, would not believe something which I knew could not be so. Because I never saw him, you see? There are some things which happen to us which the intelligence and the senses refuse just as the stomach sometimes refuses what the palate has accepted but which digestion cannot compass -- "* (151).

Rosa's denial of Bon's death, then, is a mental *vomiting*. And the novel makes only one other reference to this sort of physical reaction. This is during the scene (29-30) in which Sutpen fights his slaves for the benefit of his guests, and Henry, forced to watch, cannot bear the sight of his father covered with *blood*, and falls *vomiting* into the *stable filth*, from which Ellen raises him. This is also the scene in which Judith and Clytie, unknown to anyone, hide in the hayloft, calmly viewing the scene. *This scene is narrated by Rosa*, who holds some of the guests in the same contempt as she does Jones: "the very scum and riffraff who could not have approached the house itself under any other circumstances, not even from the rear," (28) and these mingled with the "gentlefolks, our own kind" (28). Rosa makes a social distinction between those of her own caste, and those who, like mating livestock, approach the house, the box, from the rear, a distinction which is arbitrary, based on appearances.

At this stage, it is necessary to treat Bon's significance to Rosa at some length. Why is it so important for her to have some tangible proof of his existence? Richard Poirier scratches the matter when he designates Rosa an "antebellum bobby soxer." To elaborate on this requires examining her description of the summer of 1860, *the "summer of wisteria"* (143). This is the time when the engagement of Judith and Bon takes place. Bon is Rosa's first love and it is a vicarious love: Rosa never actually sees Bon; her attention centers around the photograph *"upon a littered dressing table yet bowered and dressed (or so I thought) with all the maiden and invisible lily roses"* (147). The *"littered* dressing table" implies clutter, or trash and filth, or fertility, as in the offspring of animals. The lily rose is an imaginary flower which condenses the lily, with its connotations of purity and death, and the rose, which connotes love and sexuality. These flowers, *"maiden and invisible,"* imply something imaginary, something denied, something repressed, and they both "bower" (bedroom, place of nakedness and sexual union) and "dress" the photograph. The "littered table" is actual enough, but the photograph thereon is enshrined in a linguistic construction, a sublimation, something which is not on the table but in Rosa's mind, something true and not true of the face itself:

> *Why did I not invent, create it? -- And I know this: If I were God I would invent out of this seething turmoil we call progress something (a machine perhaps) which would adorn the barren mirror alters of every plain girl who breathes with such as this -- which is so little since we want so little -- this pictured face. It would not even need a skull behind it; almost anonymous, it would only need vague inference of some walking flesh desired by someone else even if only in some shadow-realm of make-believe* (147).

Love is transferred to the image instead of the living body; everyone knows that the production of such images is big business. Life-sized posters of attractive entertainers are widely available, and produced by the tens of thousands; they depict those who live and love in movies and television shows, the shadow-realm extraordinaire. That Rosa describes this trade in flesh as an act of God, identifying not incidentally herself with the deity, implies an unconscious link between commerce and religion; as Brown states: "the ideal type of the modern economy retains, at its very heart, the structure of the archaic sacred." (LD, 240), and Rosa's religious consciousness bears the mark of the slave-based economy of Yoknapatawpha, which also traffics in human flesh. This archetypal connection becomes more deeply relevant in relation to Rosa when we note that she is the daughter of a puritanical merchant, and her reason for staying at Sutpen's Hundred that summer is that her father is *"away on business,"* and she suspects that *"My father chose Ellen as a refuge for me because at that time Thomas Sutpen was also absent."(145)*.

Here, as on the day of the funeral, Rosa cannot believe in the actuality of Bon's existence: *'But I never saw* [his face]. *I do not even know of my own knowledge that Ellen ever saw it, that Judith ever loved it, that Henry slew it"* (147). Again, the repression of death is evident, and since the dead man and the lover are the same, sexuality is repressed also. But, as her desire is transferred onto not the man but the photographic image, "painted on the veil", it already exists in a state of death.

Rosa denies the existence of the lover, and thus denies also her capacity to love anything other than a shadow. Thus her struggle to validate Bon's reality coincides with a struggle to validate her own existence as a ghostly spectator of the invisible: *"Oh no, I was not spying while I dreamed in the lurking harborage of my own shrub or vine as I believed she dreamed upon the nooky seat which held the invisible imprint of his absent thighs just as the obliterating sand, the million finger nerves of frond and leaf the very sun and moony constellations which had looked down at him, the circumambient air, held somewhere yet his foot, his passing shape, his face, his speaking voice, his name: Charles Bon, Charles Good, Charles husband-soon-to-be"* (148). This is a complex passage, simultaneously revealing and concealing an extended web of associations. Sexual imagery (the *"nooky seat,"* the *"absent thighs"*) hides beneath the lush imagery of the garden; Rosa denies her own spectatorship, projecting this onto the foliage (described earlier as listening in on the lovers' conversation; here as having a sense of touch: the *"million finger-nerves"* and on celestial bodies: *"the sun and moony constellations,"* here compounding separate things in the manner of her creation of the *"lily roses"* in a sublimated image to which she ascribes knowledge of the real man, who is replaced in the name, which through rhythmic repetition is transformed into the bridegroom, within this social context the legitimate despoiler of the virgin.

Rosa identifies with both the male and female lovers; her thoughts of Judith bear homoerotic overtones: "[I was] *child enough to go to her and say 'Let me sleep with you'; woman enough to say 'Let us lie in bed together while you tell me what love is,' yet who did not do it . . .*" (145). Again, Rosa presents a scene as though it actually happened, then denies its reality. In this case, she projects herself into a position occupied by Clytie: *"(So I have heard) she and Judith even slept together, in the same room but with Judith in the bed and she on the floor ostensibly. But I have heard how on occasion Ellen has found them both on the pallet, and once in the bed together"* (140). This passage shows the two girls in an arrangement which is common for Faulkner's children: the white child sleeping in the bed with the black playmate sleeping on the pallet on the floor; to move from pallet to bed or bed to pallet implies on unconscious shift from one racial status to another. For Judith and Clytie to sleep together combines in the unconscious homosexuality, miscegenation, and incest. Sundquist posits the reciprocal identification of miscegenation and incest as the deepest horror in the collective experience of the South; for the white Southerner, the deepest fear is that one's blood might be tainted with black. The horror of miscegenation is also connected with the horror of bestiality; this stemming from the paradox by which the slave is simultaneously regarded as livestock and lover. Significantly, Rosa omits telling of Sutpen's original miscegenation which begot Clytie; the repression of this fact makes it all the more forcefully shocking when Mr. Compson reveals that "two of the niggers in the wagon that day were women" (61), whom Sutpen purchased in the same manner as one purchases livestock.

Rosa recalls the image of Judith and Clytie in bed in response to her recollection of another intimacy between the two sisters from which she is excluded, and the terror she feels when Clytie prevents her from advancing to the room where Charles Bon lies dead. Here, Clytie assumes the prerogative of a white woman by addressing her a "Rosa" instead of "Miss Rosa," *as Quentin in fact does.* In her recollection of this, Rosa produces some strange imagery: "the two of us joined by that hand and arm which held us, like a fierce rigid umbilical cord, twin sistered to that fell darkness which had produced her" (140).

Images of homosexuality and the womb combine in Rosa's strangest fantasy:

[I was] *fourteen, four years younger than Judith's moment which only virgins know: when the entire delicate spirit's bent is one anonymous climaxless epicene and unravished nuptial- not that widowed and nightly violation by the inescapable and scornful dead which is the meed of twenty and thirty and forty, but a world filled with living marriage like the light and air which she breathes. But it was not summer of a virgin's itching discontent; no summer's caesarean lack which should have torn me, dead flesh or even embryo, from the living: or else, by fiction's ravishing of the male-furrowed meat, also weaponed and panoplied as a man instead of hollow woman* (145).

This passage condenses a great deal of material, commencing with the onset of menstruation, the "moment which only virgins know," which apparently happens to Rosa during the Summer of 1860, a moment which she identifies with an "unravished nuptial", such as that of Judith and Bon. This image also identifies menstrual bleeding with the bleeding of the broken hymen, which, by spilling on the bed, evokes Bon's death wound. Here, Eros is merged with Death, and the scene moves into an image of necrophilia which recapitulates the fantastic erotic history of Rosa' adult life. Next comes the strangest image of all, the stillbirth by caesarean, which grows out of Rosa's fantasy on the preceding page that her childhood was spent within the womb, gestating, or buried underground. Clearly, death is equated with the state prior to birth, and anyone acquainted with *Beyond the Pleasure Principle* is aware that the fundamental desire to repeat this latter experience is the basis of the Death Instinct. Rosa's fantasy culminates with an image of male homosexual copulation, with Rosa, through the proxy of fiction, equipped with the male genitalia and performing the masculine role.

Brown (LD 119) equates the castration complex of the male child with the penis-envy of the female, an event which marks the passage into adult sexuality and "is the key to human neurosis.' He posits the cause of this phenomenon in the child's gaining awareness of sexual differentiation, the awareness that the male has the penis, while the female does not, a fact which the child believes to be due to castration, and thus we might speculate that menstrual bleeding is identified with the bleeding of the castrated one. For Rosa, the realization of sexual difference must have involved Henry, the only male playmate of her childhood. In this passage, Rosa fantastically possesses the penis, and male and female are interfused, the heterosexual relationship being subverted by the word "also." Rosa describes the male organ as a "weapon"; this evokes the image the war her father died opposing and which she lives by glorifying; also the gun with which Henry kills Bon, an act which, as Irwin suggests, is the consummation of a homoerotic love. Appropriately, the text recommences, *"It was the summer after that first Christmas that Henry brought him home." (145).*

This moment leads in two directions: forward, to the day of Bon's death, and also backward, to Rosa's childhood. She is intensely anxious as Bon is *nailed* into a *box* and placed beneath the ground. Here, the slang connotations of "nailed" (sexual intercourse) and "box' (female genitalia) are significant; in the unconscious, Bon, the lover, is returned to the womb. And the blood which Rosa sees on the mattress, which *"could have come from anywhere"* has a number of fantastic sources: 1) a slaughtered animal, which, by being in bed, could be identified with a bestial act; we have already noted Rosa's intense aversion to the slaughter of livestock and the role of bestiality in the horror of miscegenation, 2) from the vagina, either through menstruation or the breaking of the hymen by the husband, and 3) castration. Consciously, however, the blood comes from the death-wound of Charles Bon; the fusion of dead man and lover is further intensified.

The outlines of Rosa's neurosis must be completed by examining the household in which she grows up, and relating this to all that has gone before. Here, we are working with material that is more deeply repressed; therefore we must rely more on facts given by Mr. Compson and by Quentin in order to reconstruct it.

In this context, Rosa's fantasy of being torn from the womb is an expression not only of the birth trauma, but of guilt over being born at all. Mr. Compson narrates the circumstances: " [she was] born into her parents middle age (her mother must have been at least forty and she died in that childbed and Miss Rosa never forgave her father for it) at a time when . . . the family wanted only peace and quiet and probably did not expect and did not even want another child. But she was born, at the price of her mother's life, and was not permitted to forget it. She was by the same spinster aunt . . . to see in the fact of her own breathing not only the lone justification for the sacrifice of her mother's life, not only a living and walking reproach to her father, but a breathing indictment, ubiquitous and even transferable, of the entire male principle (that principle which had left the aunt a virgin at thirty-five)" (59-60). This upbringing is in itself a negation of the living body of Rosa and therefore sufficient to subordinate life to death. Here, birth and reproduction are equated with death, and the sexual act which engenders her is an act of murder. The aunt identifies the living child with the abstract and Apollonian principles of justice and retribution, perhaps sublimating her anger over her own erotic barrenness; Rosa learns to see herself as an abstraction and repeats by her own life her aunt's spinsterhood. This might be the result of another repetition which hinges on another family relationship. From the moment of birth, Rosa *is herself the aunt* of Judith and Henry. Much of the aunt's anger is projected on the marriage of her niece, Ellen, and Thomas Sutpen, and Rosa is also to repeat the role of the unwed aunt of the married niece in the relation to Judith and Charles.

After the death of the mother, the aunt assumes the role of housekeeper and thus becomes a surrogate wife to her brother, an unconsciously incestuous role which Rosa assumes in relation to her father after the aunt's elopement; Rosa even takes to wearing the aunt's discarded clothes. She thus finds herself in a love relationship to "the father she hated without knowing it" (60). Goodhue Coldfield is a man of scrupulous morality, who, within the context of Ellen's marriage, was lured into committing a questionable act which provides Thomas Sutpen with the means to furnish his mansion, which Quentin describes as something about a bill of lading, some way he persuaded Mr. Coldfield to use his credit: one of those things that when they work you were smart and when they don't you change your name and move to Texas" (259). Coldfield could have become rich from the deal; instead he refuses his share of the profits and provides only a house which Rosa keeps by "that first principle of penury which is to scrimp and save for the sake of scrimping and saving" (156), and eventually leaves his daughter destitute when during the war he closes up his store and finally nails himself into the attic to die. During his immurement, this man, whose view of religion is one of balancing accounts in a cosmic ledger (84), is one for whom Rosa is responsible for "feeding in secret and at night and with the food which in quantity was scarcely sufficient for one, the man whom she hated." The horror of this experience accounts for Rosa's aversion to the building more adequately than any feelings of prudery over sexual connotations of the word "box". But these overtones persist; the night her father is "nailed in the box" is the night she begins her "fiction's ravishing" by beginning the composition of a series of "odes to the Southern soldiers in that portfolio which when your grandfather saw it in 1885 contained a thousand or mare" (83), and she transfers her ambivalent feelings toward her father onto Thomas Sutpen, at this time an illustrious war hero, and the man who bested her father twenty years previously. Sutpen, the negation of her father's abstract principles and the man she was raised to hate, originates from the River, from the gamblers and horse-traders whom Rosa despises. The experience of her aunt's elopement with a horse- trader is traumatic for Rosa, as it thrusts her into the quasi- incestuous relationship to her father whom she despises. For Rosa, the figure of Sutpen combines the brutality she attributes to men like Jones with the omnipotence of the father in the monstrous and demonic figure she sees him as. This stands behind the bestial overtones of his proposition to Rosa, which repeats his quasi-bestial relationship to relationship to Clytie's mother, one of the original "wild niggers" who is seen as livestock, as less than human. This proposal, which condenses and confronts Rosa with the full horror of death and incest, miscegenation and bestiality, for her, the only logical response is the "indominatable outrage" which lasts into 1909.

Ellen's dying injunction that Rosa protect Judith and Henry, a responsibility which weighs so heavily on her, amounts to a psychological red herring, which connects nothing, reveals nothing, and resolves nothing. It serves Rosa as the limit which keeps the whole Apollonian dream-structure intact. Rosa's allegiance to Apollo and hatred of Dionysus is manifested in her participation in a dream which replaces life and decrees for perpetual tribute to be paid to the dead. This limit conceals from Rosa the massive complex, which reveals itself in the story of her life which she tell to Quentin in yet another fictional ravishing. The story is, as we have seen, structured like a dream, and it speaks in the language of the unconscious, the language of condensation and displacement. If life is a story which we tell to ourselves, then Rosa's life itself is a dream or nightmare from which she cannot awake.

The Extremes of Sublimation, Part 2

Harvard

"Mathematics," says Bertrand Russell, "rightly viewed, possesses not only truth, but supreme beauty - a beauty cold and austere, like that of sculpture, without any appeal to our weaker nature . . . the true spirit of delight, the exaltation, the sense of being more than man, which is the touchstone of the highest excellence, is to be found in mathematics as surely as in poetry." And, like the doctrine of the soul distinct from the body, sublimation as an attempt to be more than man, aims at immortality. "I shall not altogether die," says Horace; "My sublimations will exalt me to the stars (Brown, "Apollo and Dionysus" in LD 157).

Apollo is at once the god of all plastic powers and the soothsaying god. He who is etymologically the "lucent" one, the god of light, reigns also over the fair illusion of our inner world of fantasy. The perfection of these conditions in contrast to our imperfectly understood waking reality, as well as our profound awareness of nature's healing powers during the interval of sleep and dream, furnishes a symbolic analog to the soothsaying faculty and quite generally to the arts, which make life possible and worth living. But the image of Apollo must incorporate that thin line which the dream image may not cross, under penalty of becoming pathological, of imposing itself on us as crass reality: a discreet limitation, a freedom from all extravagant urges, the sapient tranquility of the plastic god. (Nietzsche, BT 21).

…the two of them, whether they knew it or not, in the cold room (it was quite cold now) dedicated to that best of ratiocination which after all was a good deal like Sutpen's morality and Miss Coldfield's demonizing - this room not only dedicated to it but set aside for it and suitably so since it would be here above any other place that it (the logic and morality) could do the least amount of harm - (AA 280).

The University is the apotheosis of mind, the naked stony ridge of abstraction, cold and severe, a concentration of the sublime through which the stars shine unremittingly, a place utterly hostile to life. The end of sublimation is, as we have seen, death; hence, the University is dedicated to death, and the campus is a nekropolis, a repository where what is most deadly is held, like toxic waste, in isolation from the general environment. The dormitory at Harvard, like the institution and the New England winter, is a cold and austere environment, and "this snug monastic coign, this dreamy and heatless alcove of what we call the best of thought" (258) is the domain of Apollo, the school of the elevation of spirit. It is also the "damn icebox" (292), a term which reverberates against the coffin in which Charles Bon lies "dead as beef", against Rosa's husband, the "abstract carcass of grief and outrage", against Thomas Sutpen at the slave market in Memphis, against the begetting of Clytie with the "wild nigger," against the mare which Sutpen values above Milly Jones and their newborn daughter. The carcass, with its undertones of bestiality and cannibalism, the nightmares lying behind the southern ego, is meat which paradoxically consumes the living body. In the University, the body is purely incidental, Hopkins' "bone-house, mean-house" of the far-darting Mind, "Man's mounting spirit"; the body is wasted, useless, and cast aside, so that the Mind may stride through space and time gigantically, transcending the limits of human life, becoming more than human, ruling and ruining the whole earth, like Sutpen ruling and ruining his plantation.

> Only in the latest of his tellings of the story, in *Moses and Monotheism* does Freud distinguish the brotherhood from the natural relation among the sons inside the family. In that version the brotherhood comes into being after the sons are expelled from the family, when they "club together" in the wilderness; the social contract perpetuates "the attachment that had grown up among them during the time of their exile." They club together in the fatherless wilderness; it is a fraternity of young men in college, away from home. The artifice that makes the brotherhood, the social contract, is initiation. (Brown, "Liberty" in LB 10).

Quentin and Shreve, living together in the same room like brothers found in exile, "facing each other across the lamplit table on which lay the fragile Pandora's box of scrawled paper which had filled with violent and unratiocinitive djinns and demons this snug monastic coign" (258); Nietzsche's Doric civilization confronting the arrival of the barbaric Dionysian rites in which "all the savage urges of the mind were unleashed on those occasions until they reached a paroxysm of lust and cruelty which has always struck me as the 'witches' cauldron' *par excellence"* (BT 25-26); in either case the arrival of the irrational, violent, uncontrollable force into the calm and ordered dream-temple of Apollo, the arrival of the alien, the invader from the strange land, Thomas Sutpen riding into Jefferson, "- the two of them back to back as though at the last ditch saying No to Quentin's Mississippi shade who in life had acted and reacted to the minimum of logic and morality, who dying had escaped it completely, who dead remained not only indifferent but impervious to it, somehow a thousand times more potent and alive" (280), the two brothers heroically resisting even as the world is plunged into chaos and contradiction.

Teller and tale; living and dead; distinctions thrown into doubt, and another time emerges, another college and two brothers meeting in a dorm room: Henry Sutpen and Charles Bon are drawn together at the University of Mississippi in 1859. And this is the scene which invades the dorm at Harvard, this and the summer and Christmas of 1860 at Sutpen's Hundred:

> Not two of them in a New England college sitting room but one in a Mississippi library sixty years ago, with holly and mistletoe in vases on the mantel or thrust behind, crowning and garlanding with the season and time the pictures on the walls, and a sprig or so decorating the photograph, the group - mother and two children - on the desk, behind which the father sat when the son entered . . . It would not matter here in Cambridge that the time had been winter in that garden too, and hence no bloom nor leaf even if there had been someone to walk there and be seen there.. .it did not matter to them (Quentin and Shreve) anyway, who could move without moving, as free of flesh as the father who decreed and forbade, the son who denied and repudiated, the lover who acquiesced, the love who was not bereaved, and with no tedious transition from hearth to garden to saddle, who could already be clattering over the frozen

ruts of that December night and that Christmas dawn, that day of peace and cheer, of holly and goodwill and logs on the hearth; not two of them there and then either but four of them riding the two horses through the iron darkness . . . (294-95).

Teller and tale, narrator and character, then and now, here and there, the passing of seasons, the living and dead, the North and South: the visual distinctions, the signposts by which consciousness, by which the ego, differentiates itself, degenerate, and the situation at Harvard approaches the condition of the unconscious, of archetype, of myth.

> Freud's myth of the rebellion of the sons against the father in the primal, prehistoric horde is not a historical explanation of origins, but a supra-historical archetype; eternally recurrent; a myth; an old, old story. … Freud seems to project into prehistoric times the constitutional crisis of seventeenth-century England. The primal father is *absolute monarch* of the horde; the females are his *property.* The sons form a *conspiracy* to *overthrow* the despot, and in the end substitute a *social contract* with *equal rights* for all (Brown, "Liberty" 3).

> Keeping in mind this notion of revenge on a substitute, we can now understand how Quentin's act of narration in *Absalom* is an attempt to seize his father's authority by gaining temporal priority. In the struggle with his father, Quentin will prove that he is the better man by being a better narrator - he will assume the authority of an author because his father does not know the whole story, does not know the true reason for Bon's murder, while Quentin does (Irwin 119).

The story is the story of Henry and Charles, the brothers expelled from the household, wandering the streets of New Orleans and then being swept along the course of the Civil War in the University Company, discussing the taking (the rape) of their sister Judith, though this is the same act the father has forbidden; it is the story of "the band of brothers who feel the incest taboo and the lure of strange women; and adopt military organization (gang organization) for purposes of rape." ("Liberty" 15). This is the organization of the Confederate Army, whose officers are elected and can be arbitrarily demoted by their own troops, "who would whip three separate armies in as many days and then tear down their own fences to cook meat robbed from their own smokehouses, who on one night and with a handful of men would gallantly set fire to and destroy a million dollar garrison of enemy supplies and on the next night be discovered by a neighbor in bed with his wife and be shot to death' (346). The Confederate Army is fraternally structured; Brown equates this structure with the politics of juvenile delinquency ('Liberty" 15).

But behind the fraternity stands the figure of the deposed father: 'Here is the contradiction in liberty, equality, and fraternity, sonship and brotherhood are espoused against fatherhood: but without a father there can be no sons or brothers. Locke's sons, like Freud's, cannot free themselves from father psychology, and are crucified by the contradictory commands issuing from the Freudian super-ego, which says both 'thou shalt be like the father,' and 'thou shalt not be like the father,' that is, many things are his prerogative. Fraternal organization covertly assumes a father; ego-organization covertly assumes a super-ego." ("Liberty" 5-6). Therefore, Colonel Sutpen has a trump to play, and has the prerogative of summoning Henry to his tent in the night to prevent once and for all the incestuous marriage. The shadow of the father is present at Harvard as well: Quentin thinks: *"yes, we are both Father. Or maybe Father and I are both Shreve, maybe it took Father and me both to make Shreve or Shreve and me both to make Father or maybe Thomas Sutpen to make all of us"* (261-62). The wrestling of Charles/Shreve and Henry/Quentin in the "tomblike room" (346) over the question of incest is a re-enactment of "what Freud calls the primal scene; their wrestling is sexual as well as aggressive, an imitation of the parental copulation." ("Liberty" 25). The outcome of this is fratricidal war, civil war: "There are always two brothers: Romulus and Remus, Cain and Abel, Osiris and Set; and one of them murders the other." ("Liberty" 26).

"It is the tale of Shem and Shaun in North Armorica. "Bostonians sometimes seemed to love violence for its own sake. Over the years there had developed a rivalry between the South End and the North End of the City. On Pope's Day, November 5, when parades were held to celebrate the defeat of Guy Fawkes' famous gunpowder plot, the rivalry between the two sections broke out into a free-for-all with stones and barrel-staves the principle weapons. The two sides even developed a semi-military organization with recognized leaders, and of late the fighting had become increasingly bloody." ("Liberty" 30).

For Quentin, the rebellion against the father in the form of narrative superiority is necessarily what we are calling a violation of the Apollonian limit, for, as John T. Matthews demonstrates, what the elder Compson offers his son through his telling of the Sutpen drama, is a way to continue living when life becomes worthless, a vehicle by which Quentin might rid himself, that is project, the elements of his psychological torment: his obsession with his sister Candace's virginity which is told in *The Sound and the Fury,* the loss of his family's high station in the community, and the finality of death. Mr. Compson suggests the possibility of creating, of inscribing significance in a universe devoid of absolute meaning, or in the terminology of Nietzsche, the fair and healing illusions "which make life possible and worth living" (BT 21), in the terminology of Brown, to deal with the dilemma of incest and morbidity, the contradiction of Eros and Thanatos, through sublimation.

But Quentin's superior knowledge of the Sutpen tale is based precisely on its literalization, he having gained it when he and Rosa make the journey to Sutpen's Hundred, meet and preside over the deaths of the actual Clytie and the actual Henry. Here Quentin learns the true identity of Charles Bon, and the fantasy of incest imposes itself as the gross fact of the relationship between Bon and Judith, and fratricide as the fact between Bon and Henry. In the end, Quentin is left in the cold room at Harvard, in an environment of "academic orthodoxy, senile and senatorial, [which] is against fraternities; . . . against athletics; against play; against sex; against youth." ("Liberty" 14) In the dark, Shreve assaults Quentin with the full horror of the story, as Quentin lies in bed "thinking 'Nevermore of peace. Nevermore of peace. Nevermore Nevermore Nevermore" (373).

Graveyard

Now, once a tribe member has a proper name, he can in a sense be recreated in his absence. 'He' can be thought about, using 'thought' here in a special non-conscious sense of fitting into language structures. While there had been earlier graves of a sort, occasionally somewhat elaborate, this is the first age in which we find ceremonial graves as a common practice. If you think of someone close to you who has died, and then suppose that he or she had no name, in what would your grief consist? How long could it last? Previously, man, like other primates, had probably left his dead where they fell, or else hidden them from view with stones, or in some instances roasted and eaten them. But just as a noun for an animal makes that relationship a more intense one, so a name for a person. And when the person dies, the name still goes on, and hence the relationship, almost as in life, and hence burial practices and mourning. (Jaynes 136).

And in the magic-dirt complex we can discern the fear of death and the fantastic wish for an immortal self-replenishing body. Hence the rituals of scatophagy, necrophagy, and the more generally constant association of dirt with funeral ceremonies. Priam, on the death of Hector, rolled in the dung heap; primitive tribes smear themselves as a sign of mourning, and we wear black; the Tonga Islanders raised a pious mound of ordure on the grave; our Indo-European ancestors raised a mound of stones.(Brown, "Filthy Lucre" in LD 300).

Quentin was not aware yet of just where they were because he had been riding with his head lowered against the drizzle, until he looked up into the rain like melting gold and saw the grove, the clump of cedars on the crest of the hill, dissolving into the rain as if the trees had been drawn in ink on a wet blotter - the cedars beyond which, beyond the ruined fields, beyond which, would be the oak grove and the gray huge rotting deserted house half a mile away (AA 187).

This is the entry of the sacred ground, the cedars and melted gold of the temple, wealth concentrated in stones. This is the necropolis, the graveyard, the final plantation of the Sutpen Family. The stone is immortal, as Judith Compson observes: "the block of stone cant be *is* because it never can become *was* because it can't ever die or perish . . ." (127-28) The stone, neither living or dead, stands in relation to the living man as a Derridaean supplement: it both recalls the absent life and replaces this life precisely by keeping the name of the dead on the tongue of the living; to name is to remember. But Thomas Sutpen's stone replaces him before he has even died; his troops who transport his stone and Ellen's refer to the marble slabs as "Colonel" and "Mrs. Colonel" (189). The stone is sculpted and therefore Apollonian, an image and an illusion, like the photograph of Charles Bon. Likewise the name is a fragile illusion: "Charles Husband-soon-to-be" (148), and "Thomas Sutpen, Colonel, 23rd Mississippi Infantry, C.S.A." (188). In each case, the title, the role, is forever fixed and inviolate, yet forever meaningless. This double constitution stands as a metaphor for the Sutpen's wealth and position, which was in 1860 as seemingly strong and secure as possible. Nietzsche cites Schopenhauer's metaphor for the seemingly solid and irrevocable image of Apollo, the "man caught in the veil of Maya: "even as on an immense, raging sea, assailed by huge wave crests, a man sits in a little rowboat trusting his frail craft, so amidst the furious torments of the world, the individual sits tranquilly, supported by the *principium individuationis* and relying on it." (BT 22). Likewise, the Sutpens become caught in their own veil of Maya: Mansion and cotton, chattel and slaves, and the son in college as the daughter's engagement to the gentleman from New Orleans is arranged, even as storm and flood gather, 'when the destiny of Sutpen's family which for twenty years now had been like a lake welling from quiet springs into a quiet valley and spreading, rising almost imperceptibly and in which the four members of it floated in sunny suspension, felt the first subterranean movement toward the outlet, the gorge which would be the land's catastrophe too, and the four peaceful swimmers turning suddenly to face one another, not yet with alarm or distrust but just alert, feeling the dark set, none of them yet at that point where man looks about at his companions in disaster and thinks *When will I stop trying to save them and save only myself? (74).*

By *1865,* the mansion is a hull of its former splendor: the fields untended, the chattel consumed, the slaves fled, son and fiancé gone, the daughters in rags. The society on which Sutpen's Hundred rests is staggering from war, defeat, and occupation.

To recall those whose names are engraved in stone is to enter into what Eliot calls "Death's Dream Kingdom" (The Hollow Men 1.20), a privilege bought at the expense of the living. There is an economy in which the desires and comforts of the living are exchanged for the lifeless phallic marble, the sublime figure of the human rebellion against death, The journal of this economy, written not in the letters but in the blank surfaces of the stones, is read aloud by Mr. Compson to his son. The first two stones, those of Thomas and Ellen, were paid for by the sailors who "got them past a seacoast so closely blockaded that the incoming runners refused any cargo except ammunition," and by Sutpen's "ragged and starving troops without shoes watching that dark interdict ocean across which a grim lightless solitary ship held within its hold two thousand precious pounds- space containing not bullets, not even something to eat, but that much bombastic and and inert carven rock which for the next year was to be a part of the regiment, to follow it into Pennsylvania and be present at Gettysburg, moving behind the regiment in a wagon driven by the demon's body servant through swamp and plain and mountain pass, the regiment moving no faster than the wagon could, with starved gaunt men and gaunt spent horses knee deep in icy mud or snow, sweating and cursing it through bog and morass like a piece of artillery" (189).

The stone of Charles Bon is bought "with that money [Judith] got when she sold the store" (190), the store which Thomas Sutpen opened after his return, from which he purchased his own death with the ribbons and the candy with which he purchased Milly Jones, and alignment of commerce and death which echoes the suspicion that the whole unconscious aim of the mercantile economy is the financing of the family monument, the purchase of immortality. The acquisition of this stone is for Judith the acceptance of obligation of Bon's son Etienne, who "had produced complete and subject to no microbe in that cloyed and scented maze of shuttered silk, as if he were a delicate and perverse spirit-symbol" (196), one forbidden to touch the earth or see the sun, taken "into that gaunt and barren household where his very silken remaining clothes, his delicate shirt and stockings and shoes which still remained to remind him of what he had once been, vanished, fled from his arms and body and legs as if they had been woven of chimaeras or smoke" (197), who is fitted "beneath that harsh and shapeless denim cut to an iron pattern and sold by the millions' (196), who was "guarded as if he were a Spanish virgin" (200), who came from a place "where the very abstractions which he might have observed -- monogamy and fidelity and decorum and gentleness and affection -- were as purely rooted in the flesh's offices as the digestive process" (199), who went down "the thorny and flint-paved path toward the Gethsemane which he had decreed and created for himself, where he had crucified himself" (209), and who in between worked "the savage steel-and-wood male symbol, ripping from the prone rich female earth corn to feed them both." (200)

Judith's obligation is at its core a family obligation, though Etienne has no clear place in the family: "the child might be Clytie's, got by its father on the body of his own daughter" (201), or *"I will tell them that you are Henry's son and who could or would dare to dispute"*, and finally *"Call me Aunt Judith, Charles"* (208). Etienne is in fact Judith's nephew, the son of her brother who would also have been her husband, "And how Clytie must have lived during the next twelve years while she raised the child who had been born in an old slave cabin and scrimped and saved the money to finish paying out for the stone on which Judith had paid [Quentin's] grandfather the hundred dollars twenty-four years ago and which, when his grandfather tried to refuse it, she (Clytie) set the rusty can full of nickles and dimes and frayed paper money on the desk and walked out of the office without a word" (210).

Quentin views the final tombstone, Judith's, hearing his father speak:

> *Beautiful lives women live - women do. In very breathing they draw meat and drink from some beautiful attenuation of unreality in which the shades and shapes of facts -- of which birth and bereavement, of suffering and bewilderment and despair -- move with the substanceless decorum of lawn party charades. . . . Miss Rosa ordered that one. She decreed that headstone of Judge Benbow. He had been the executor of her father's estate, appointed by no will since Mr. Coldfield left neither will nor estate except the house and the rifled shell of the store. So he appointed himself, elected himself probably out of some conclave of neighbors and citizens who left baskets of food on her doorstep at night, the dishes (the plate containing the food, the napkins which covered it) from which she never washed but returned soiled to the empty basket and set the basket back on the same step where she found it as if to*

carry out completely the illusion that it had never existed or at least she had never touched, emptied it, . . . who doubtless tasted the food, criticized its quality or cooking, chewed and swallowed it and felt it digest yet still clung to that delusion, that calm incorrigible insistence that that which all incontrovertible evidence tells her is so does not exist, as women can -- that same self deluding which declined to admit that the liquidation of the store had left her something, that she had been left anything but a complete pauper, she would not accept the actual money from the sale from Judge Benbow yet would accept the money's value (and after a few years, over-value) in a dozen ways . . . he, Benbow had in his office a portfolio, a fat one, with Estate of Goodhue Coldfield. Private *written across it in indelible ink. After the Judge died his son Percy opened it. It was filled with racing forms and cancelled betting tickets on horses whose very bones were no man knew where now* (211-12).

Judith's stone is bought with a mythic trust of guilt. It is an illusion bought with the illusion of an illusion, for which the Judge continues to pay for the remainder of his life.

The five names, Thomas and Ellen Sutpen, Charles Bon, Charles Etienne St. Valéry Bon, Judith Sutpen, inscribed on the five gravestones, constitute the most enduring form of Sutpen's design, the form that outlasts all other ways of memory, the sublime symbol, and the ultimate immortal family. In the last shrine of Apollo and death, Dionysus comes as the wild card which ruins the pure ideal, the white family, the dynasty of stainless blood. For it is here that the merging which Sutpen tried to prevent takes place; here he has his son and grandson, not within the conscious and white family the graveyard was intended to immortalize, but from within the dark family, the repressed children, the family of unfettered desire.

"Shall I at least set my lands in order?"

Quentin's Quest for the Fatal Grail

The common area between Nietzsche and Brown is the eschatological motive which underlies the work of both. In the opening section of *Life Against Death* , aptly titled "The Problem," Brown states:

> …psychoanalysis offers a theoretical framework for exploring the possibility of a way out of the nightmare of endless "progress and endless Faustian discontent, a way out of the human neurosis, a way out of history. . . . If historical consciousness is finally transformed into psychoanalytical consciousness, the grip of the dead hand of the past on life in the present world would be loosened, and man would be ready to live instead of making history, to enjoy instead of paying back old scores and debts, and to enter that state of Being which is the goal of his Becoming (19).

The quest for a viable eschatological possibility continues as a common concern for Brown through the conclusion of the chapter "Apollo and Dionysus":

> If there is a "way out" from the dialectic of cumulative repression, guilt, and aggression, it must lie not in sublimation but in an alternative to sublimation. To understand our present predicament we have to go back to its origins, to the beginning of Western civilization and to the Greeks, who taught and still teach us how to sublimate, and who worshipped the god of sublimation, Apollo (124).

At this point, Brown refers to and echoes *The Birth of Tragedy* which likewise searches "the desolate of present-day culture" for the possibility of a "sound, healthy future" (123). Nietzsche expresses this possibility as a venient immanence of Dionysus:

> But what amazing change is wrought in that gloomy desert of our culture by the wand of Dionysus. All that is half-alive, rotten, broken and stunted by the whirlwind he wraps in a cloud of red dust and

carries off like a vulture. Our distracted eyes look for all that has vanished and are confused, for what they see has risen from beneath the earth into the golden light, so full and green, so richly alive. In the midst of all this life, joy, and sorrow, tragedy sits in noble ecstasy, listening to a sad, distant song which tells of the mothers of being, whose names are Wish, Will, and Woe (123-24).

These passages form a perfect analogy to what *Absalom*'s interpreters virtually unanimously view as the central problem facing Quentin Compson, and by extension the South, heirs to Thomas Sutpen's "Faustian discontent," oppressed by "the dead hand of the past." The interpretation of Faulkner, then, must confront the eschatological question, that is, the possibility of gaining freedom from the condition which we have analyzed in the previous chapters, the possibility of "an alternative to sublimation," of the renewal of the Waste Land.

I

The analog of the Waste Land has intrigued numerous commentators of the novels of William Faulkner. *In William Faulkner: The Yoknapatawpha Country* , Cleanth Brooks titles his chapter on *Sartoris* "The Waste Land: Southern Exposure," setting this title over and against the meaninglessness and monotony, the barrenness and ineffectuality which marks the lives of those returning from the war in Europe in 1919, seeing in the character of Horace Benbow " a less sophisticated J. Alfred Prufrock," one of "Eliot's deracinated young men among the Boston teacups or the protagonist of *The Waste Land* walking along the autumn-stricken Thames?! *(105-6)* James E. Miller, in his essay "Sanctuary: Yoknapatawpha's Waste Land," notes a parallel between Eliot's figure of Tiresias, who witnesses the seduction of the Typist, and Faulkner's blind man who witnesses Popeye's rape of Temple Drake, and the parallel between Faulkner's old white fortune-teller and Eliot's Madam Sosostris, both of whom "represent an energy, integrity, and earnestness (however superstitious) that have disappeared from religious belief" (153). Edmund Volpe, in *A Reader's Guide to William Faulkner*, while noting the thematic similarities between *The Waste Land* and *The Sound and the Fury* says, in a way which suggests the idea of the Grail, of the latter: "It encompasses the degeneration of a family and of a society, becoming like Eliot's poem a revelation of the spiritual state of modern man. In the final section, Dilsey's response to the Easter sermon is used by Faulkner to communicate the feeling, without ever stating the idea, that human compassion is what modern man has lost and what he must recover to achieve regeneration" (96). Ida Fasel, in her article "A 'Conversation' between Faulkner and Eliot," shows that "the effect of Eliot on Faulkner was an efflorescence, as when the Elizabethans expanded by hundreds of lines Ovid's slenderly told stories" (206) by arraying lines and phrases from *The Waste Land* in one column, and in a parallel column presenting a corresponding citation from or allusion to *The Sound and the Fury*. The result is a fascinating and effective series of resonances and harmonies which the reader apprehends in the blank space between the columns. I offer here a small sample of this remarkable and imaginative piece:

Looking into the heart of light	He was just looking at the fire (68). Light fascinates Benjy: (B7, 11, 27, 70,77).
Neither/Living nor dead	Any live man is better than any dead man but no live man or dead man is very much better than any other live or dead man (Q 175).
Madam Sostris	"I seed de beginning, en now I sees de endin" (iv, 371).
your card	single blind turn of the card (Q 221).
drowned Phoenician sailor	Quentin.
pearls . . . his eyes	The eyes will come floating up, out of the deep quiet and the sleep (Q 144).
lady of situations	Caddy.
one-eyed merchant	Jason.
something . . . on his back	His money hoard.
forbidden to see	kept hidden.
death by water	Quentin.
crowds of people . . in a ring	I watched the crowns of people's heads (Q109).
Unreal City	Cambridge (199-200).

In "*As I Lay Dying* and *The Waste Land* - Some Relationships," Mary Jane Dickerson describes a similar series of correspondences between Faulkner and Eliot, but takes the additional step of connecting *As I Lay Dying* with the vegetation myths enumerated by Frazer in *The Golden Bough*, most specifically "an examination of *The Golden Bough* suggests that Darl may be identified with Frazer's study of the scapegoat in primitive life. Darl's family refuse to try to understand his sensitivity; indeed, they see it as a madness injurious to themselves. Frazer's discussion explains that men were sent away as scapegoats to carry the disease or evil afflicting the people with them." (132)

That Faulkner's novels should contain so many resonances with *The Waste Land* and *The Golden Bough* is hardly coincidental. Dickerson's article commences: "Certain evidence indicates that Faulkner, in writing *As I Lay Dying,* knew the vegetation myths in Frazer's *The Golden Bough.* T.S. Eliot uses Frazer in *The Waste Land* which Faulkner probably read in *The Dial* in November, 1922, prior to its publication in book form later the same year." (192) Robert M. Slabey notes that Faulkner titled a section of his *Collected Stories* "Wasteland" and a chapter of *Pylon* "Lovesong of J.A. Prufrock". Joseph Blotner confirms this by indicating in several places in his biography *William Faulkner* that the novelist had read both Eliot and Frazer in the earliest stages of his career, and had both in mind as he wrote his first novel; Blotner in fact relates that Faulkner drew on Frazer when naming his estate, Rowanoak, which was believed to be haunted by

> Judith Shegog, a beautiful girl, the story went, who fell to her death trying to elope with a Yankee officer. She was a friendly ghost, they were sure, but it was eerie to hear the faint piano notes drifting up the broad staircase in the still night.It was not fitting that their new home should still be known as the old Shegog house or the Bailey place. Faulkner had read in Frazer's *The Golden Bough* the way Scottish farmers put pieces of rowan tree over the doors of cowhouses to prevent witches from casting spells and stealing the milk. Indigenous to Scotland Faulkner named this portion of E-AhNah-Yea's land "Rowanoak," and later had it egraved on stationery in Gothic script (262).

For the sake of brevity we will not attempt an exhaustive description of the parallels which exist between the texts of Frazer and Faulkner. Since the Waste Land is a concept residing over and above this exercise, its scope within it must be controlled by the literary work which has brought the term into whatever career it will have within the critical lexicon: that is, the poetry of T. S. Eliot. In moving toward establishing a metaphorical relationship between the idea of the Vegetation Myth and Ritual and the idea of Psychoanalysis, a relation to be articulated within the intellectual space latent within the term Waste Land, we shall for the moment set our discursive parameters as consisting of 1) the anthropological works cited by Eliot as primary sources from which "not only the title, but the plan and a good deal of incidental symbolism were suggested," Jessie L. Weston's From *Ritual to Romance* and Frazer's "Adonis, Attis, Osiris" Volumes of *The Golden Bough* ; and 2) also the two Faulknerian novels which John T. Irwin discusses more or less interchangeably in light of his psychoanalytic models, *The Sound and the Fury* and *Absalom, Absalom!* . Within this space we will hazard a brief survey of the existing parallels. At this point it is necessary to keep in mind the difference between Faulknerian parallelism and the parallelism which Eliot describes in relation to *Ulysses* rather than "systematically manipulating a continuous parallel." Faulkner throughout his work consistently carries out the systematic manipulation of a discontinuous and self-subverting parallel, a conspicuous example being the distorted Christ- symbolism surrounding Joe Christmas in *Light in August*. This process of subverted parallelism is best viewed within the Freudian paradigm of the Dreamwork, a work of condensation and displacement operating in a given sector of the unconscious, a process by which the repressed is both expressed and distorted.

It is also necessary to take note of the highly intertextual system which operates within the compendium of Myth, the *Metamorphoses* or *The Golden Bough,* a system of interlocking reference in which characters and places appear in multiple narratives, much as, in *Yoknapatawpha,* Quentin Compson appears in both *The Sound and the Fury* and in *Absalom* and Thomas Sutpen in *Absalom* and in *The Unvanquished.* These multiple accounts are often fragmentary or episodic or contradictory; therefore there cannot be said to be a unitary *Myth* of Adonis or Persephone or Dionysus; these figures are rather *nexes* convergences of textual lines. Between the complex systems of Frazer and Faulkner there can be isolated, from an apparently infinite but possibly finite field of intertextual possibility, a relatively small number of well-defined but non-autonomous resonances which will achieve the most toward advancing this exercise.

1. Adonis A structure which is dreamlike within the parameters of the dreamwork structure operating within *Absalom* The figure of Adonis or Tammuz corresponds at all points with Charles Bon, the attractive stranger, "the youthful spouse or lover of Ishtar" (Frazer 379), "the comely youth beloved by Aphrodite" (Frazer 380), who dies " *A tamarisk that in the garden has drunk no water,! whose crown in the field has brought forth no blossom* (Babylonian hymn cited in Frazer 379). The death of Adonis "appears to have been annually mourned, to the shrill music of flutes, by men and women about midsummer in the month named after him, the month of Tammuz. The dirges were seemingly chanted over an effigy of the dead god, which was washed with pure water, anointed with oil, and clad in a red robe . . ." (Frazer 379); the time of year corresponds with that of the killing and funeral of Charles Bon [*"six hours of a summer afternoon saw it all* (AA 152)], dressed in a faded officer's uniform, enclosed in a wooden box, lowered under the earth, presided over by men and women: Wash Jones, Judith, Clytie, Rosa, and Theophilus McCaslin, who instead of playing the shrill flute, prays for the dead man with a rebel yell, delivering *"his old man's shrill loud cacophonous voice: 'Yaaaay, Forest! Yaaaaay, John Sartoris!* Yaaaaaay! (152). Although he is killed not by a boar but by fratricide in an altogether different archetypal situation, Charles Bon is clearly the young man who passes "away from the cheerful earth to the gloomy subterranean world, 'to the land from which there is no returning, to the house of darkness, where dust lies on door and bolt" (Frazer 379). The female figures in the myth, Ishtar and Allatu, or as they are known in Greek, Aphrodite and Persephone, when applied as parallels to their Faulknerian counterparts Judith Bon and the Octoroon, present a self-interfering problematic, a knot. Like Charles Bon, Tammuz is twice given, twice beloved, once by the goddess of love and once by the goddess of the underworld; the problem comes into play when Judith and the Octoroon are assigned to either role within the archetypal drama.

Sutpen's Hundred might correspond with the Syrian Vale of Adonis: "It was here that, according to the legend, Adonis met Aphrodite for the first and last time, and here his mangled body was buried. A fairer scene could hardly be imagined for a story of tragic love and death. . . . In antiquity the whole of the lovely vale appears to have been dedicated to Adonis, and to this day it is haunted by his memory; for the heights which shut it in are crested at various points by mined monuments of his worship " (Frazer 382) If this is the case, then it is Judith who is Aphrodite, the fair goddess and lover, and the Octoroon who rules the realm of death, the New Orleans underworld, where men engage in fatal duels, or perhaps Eulalia Bon, the cold mother who allows her son to inhabit such a place in order to advance her own ends, her own design. The marriage of Judith and Charles produces no children, cut short by an untimely death; Judith is designated by the epithet of "widowed bride (AA 22, 142), a designation which pervades the entire text of the novel. She and Clytie and Rosa live together *the busy eventless lives of three nuns in a barren and poverty-stricken convent* " (AA 155), in their own Vale of Adonis, that place of convents (Frazer 382), but Judith does not mourn. The three maidens stand over the fresh grave of the fallen youth, and walk together back to the house, and express no grief (AA, 152). And here the parallel is subverted.

The other possibility which might be considered here is that of the Octoroon as Aphrodite, who journeys to the underworld in search of her fallen lover, and Judith as Persephone, keeper of the underworld where the lover dwells. The figure of Sutpen's Hundred, no longer bound with the Vale of Adonis but now with Hades, is another epithet which permeates the text even when it is not named, and Clytie guards its entrance, *the cold Cerberus of his private hell* " (AA 136). The ritual of the three maidens weeping over the grave is repeated in 1870, when the tombstone is erected, and it is the Octoroon who weeps (AA 192). But for her, the death of her lover is not so untimely: their marriage is long since consummated; they have a son, Etienne. There is a successor. Thus one interpretive option holds at precisely that point where the other breaks down: Faulkner's Adonis can be childless, or he can be mourned, but not both. And yet both possibilities are imaginatively condensed. The interstice between novel and myth is structured like a dream, integrating a number of contradictory possibilities within a system of symbols which is fully coherent within the logic of the Freudian Dreamwork, in which the grammar of silence is the grammar of validity.

The scope of this intertextual space, this Dreamspace, is increased considerably if through a further reading of Frazer we introduce into our discussion the custom of sacred prostitution in connection with the worship of the goddess of love. Frazer tells us that "at Babylon every woman, whether rich or poor, had once in her life to submit to the embraces of a stranger at the Temple of Mylitta, that is, of Ishtar or Asarte, and to dedicate to the goddess the wages earned by this sanctified harlotry" (384), and that "At Paphos the custom of religious prostitution is said to have been instituted by King Cinyras, and to have been practiced by his daughters, the sisters of Adonis, who, having incurred the wrath of Aphrodite, mated with strangers and ended their days in Egypt" (385). These passages evoke not only the New Orleans Octoroons, "raised and trained to fulfill a woman's sole end and purpose: to love, to be beautiful, to divert" (AA 117), but even more strikingly the fate of Caddy Compson in *The Sound and the Fury,* who through her sexual promiscuity, her sleeping with strangers, is compelled to leave her home in Jefferson, never to return. The dreamspace expands still further if we include the episode of the myth in which Cinyras "is said to have begotten his son Adonis in incestuous intercourse with his daughter Myrrha" (Frazer 386). The motif of father/daughter incest is prominent in *Go Down, Moses* , in which old Carrothers McCaslin begets Terrell by his slave/daughter Tomasina, an action which influences the destiny of his family over successive generations, and appears also in *Absalom* as General Compson speculates that Etienne "might be Clytie's, got by its father on the body of his own daughter" (201). Frazer speculates that the practical basis of the widespread practice of father/daughter and brother/sister incest among ancient royalty, is control of succession. He explains,

> In countries where royal blood was traced through women only, and where consequently the king held office merely through virtue of his marriage with a hereditary princess, who was the real sovereign, it appears to have often happened that a prince married his own sister, the princess royal, in order to obtain with her hand the crown which otherwise would have gone to another man, perhaps to a stranger. May not this same rule of descent not have furnished a motive for incest with a daughter? For it seems a natural corollary from such a rule that the king was bound to vacate the throne on

the death of his wife, the queen, since he occupied it only by virtue of his marriage with her. When by that marriage terminated, his right to the throne terminated with it and passed at once to his daughter's husband. Hence if the king desired to reign after his wife's death, the only way in which he could legitimately continue to do so was by marrying his daughter, and thus prolonging through her the title which had formerly been his through her mother (386).

This paragraph, when read against the Compson/Sutpen myth, attains relevance in comparison with the attachments between Quentin and Caddy (Quentin declares the commission of incest in order to be cast into hell, where he and his sister would be alone together, where the Compson Honor would not be claimed by a stranger, a Dalton Ames or a Herbert Head, and Judith and Henry, the latter of whom "used to think that I would hate the man that I would have to look at every day and whose every move and action and speech would say to me, I have seen and touched parts of your sister's body that you will never see and touch . . ." (328). This is amplified further when placed in comparison with Thomas Sutpen, who upon the death of his wife Ellen proposes marriage by offering the dead wife's ring to his daughter-like sister-in-law, Rosa.

The father/daughter aspect of this succession through incest attains a still deeper significance when introduced to Ernest Jones' theory of the "Phantasy of reversal of generations," which is discussed in relation to Faulkner by Irwin (64-69). This is the fantasy through which the son believes he will grow up to become the parent of his father, and through which a man may identify his son with his own father. Might not this process also take place within a father/daughter relationship? Might not a man unconsciously identify his daughter with his own mother? If so, the operating model is clearly Oedipal, and the unconscious fear of mother/son incest might motivate the selection of a patriarchal mode of dynasty, as Sutpen does, when faced with the choice between creating a dynasty based on either maternal or paternal succession.

2. Attis. The outstanding feature of the myth of Attis is the god's death by self-mutilation: "he unmanned himself under a pinetree, and bled to death on the spot" (Frazer 404). This detail parallels a single striking image which Quentin narrates in *The Sound and the Fury* :

"Versh told me about a man mutilated himself. He went into the woods and did it with a razor, sitting in a ditch. A broken razor, flinging them backward over his shoulder the same motion complete the jerked skein of blood backward not looping. It's not not having them. It's never to have had them then I could say o That That's Chinese I don't know Chinese" (143). According to Frazer, "The story of the self-mutilation of Attis is clearly an attempt to account for the self-mutilation of his priests, who regularly castrated themselves on entering the service of the goddess" (404). Quentin contemplates the possibility of self-mutilation in response to his own goddess, Candace. Irwin discusses the psychological castration of Quentin in the face of the superior courage of his sister:

Since Quentin's incestuous desire for his sister is synonymous with death, it is no surprise that in the scene by the branch, where Quentin puts his knife to his sister's throat and offers to kill her and then himself, their conversation parodies that of sexual intercourse:

will you close your eyes
no like this youll have to push it harder
touch your hand to it
push it are you going to
do you want me to
yes push it
touch your hand to it

It is the mark of the brilliance and centrality of this scene that its imagery evokes as well the reason for that feat which continually unmans Quentin whenever he tries to assume the masculine role (46).

For Irwin, the fear of castration is symbolized by Quentin's dropping of the phallic knife (47). Frazer says of the identity of Attis: [he] was said to have been a fair young shepherd or herdsman beloved by Cybele, the mother of the gods, a great Asiatic goddess of fertility, who had her chief home in Phrygia. Some held it that Attis was her son" (403). Cybele is, of course, the goddess for whose sake the priests of Attis perform their ritual castration. Irwin observes, "Quentin's narcissism is linked with his incestuous desire for his sister, for as Otto

Rank points out, brother-sister incest is a substitute for child-parent incest - what the brother seeks in his sister is his mother" (43). As Irwin is well aware, castration at the hands of the father is the punishment for incest; Quentin is voluntarily carrying out upon himself the demands of a projected inner primal father. In the analysis of dreams, behind the fear of castration, there is nothing to be uncovered.

3. Osiris. The space between Osiris and Faulkner is structured like a dreamwork which is more complex than the silence between Adonis and Faulkner, operating as it does within *The Sound and the Fury* as well as *Absalom,* condensing crucial points of each novel within a single image. In this structure, the motif of brother/sister incest is a feature occupying the level of prominence of the self-mutilation motif in the Attis myth, occupying a central and visible position, rather than lying buried within the genealogy of the structured silence, as it does in the Adonis structure.

Frazer states: "Osiris was the offspring of an intrigue between the earth-god Seb and the sky-goddess Nut. . . . When the sun-god Ra perceived that his wife Nut had been unfaithful to him, he declared with a curse that she should be delivered of the child in no month and no year" (421). Charles Bon is likewise conceived and repressed, by his father Sutpen, who learns of his "negro" origins. But Charles, partly through chance and partly through the machinations of his mother Eulalia and her New Orleans lawyer, reappears through a "chance" meeting with his brother Henry at the University of Mississippi years later, just as the mother of Osiris "had another lover, the god Thoth or Hermes, as the Greeks called him, and he playing at draughts with the moon won from her a seventy-second part of each day, and having compounded five whole days out of these parts he added them to the Egyptian year of three hundred and sixty days. . . . On these five days, regarded as outside the year of twelve months, the curse of the sun-god did not rest, and accordingly Osiris was born on the first of them (Frazer 421). Just as the five days lie outside the power of Ra, the University lies outside the power of Sutpen, and the narrative which opens up in 1910, establishes the interstice inhabited by the fantastic incestuous pentad of Charles, Henry, Judith, Quentin, and Caddy. A similar pentad comes into being through the pregnancy of Nut: "on the second of the supplementary days she gave birth to the elder Horus, on the third to the god Set, whom the Greeks called Typhon, on the fourth to the goddess Isis, and on the fifth to the goddess Nephthys. Set married his sister Nephthys, and Osiris married his sister Isis" (Frazer 421). Frazer describes the horticultural achievements of this latter couple: "Isis, the sister and wife of Osiris, discovered wheat and barley growing wild, and Osiris introduced the cultivation of these grains amongst his people, who forthwith abandoned cannibalism and took kindly to a corn diet' (421). There lies a parallel here to Judith, who during the year of the war lives off whatever she can find, although this parallel is subverted by the fact that Charles never lives to be her husband and cultivate the land, and the people of that country continue their psychological cannibalism decades after his death.

According to Frazer, Osiris died through a plot of his brother Set, who tricked him into laying in a specially designed coffer, thereupon he "slammed the lid down on him, nailed it fast, soldered it with molten lead, and flung the coffer into the Nile" (422). Charles suffers fratricide through Henry, who says to him *what my sister have and are belongs to you* (AA 32), but who murders him when he attempts to claim the sister, just as Osiris died by claiming that other hollow vessel his brother gave him as a gift. Charles and Quentin (who dies by drowning in the Charles River), combine here into the figure of Osiris, just as the figure of Isis, who "sheared off a lock of her hair, put on mourning attire, and wandered disconsolately up and down, seeking the body" (Frazer 422), encompasses the characters of Judith and Caddy. Isis is the mourning traveler on the great river, the Nile, the Mississippi, in Memphis, in search of the pieces of the dismembered body. Clytie brings home Etienne, and Caddy seeks out others who will honor her brother's name. Isis entrusts the burial of the various parts of Osiris' body to a selected priesthood, to be honored as a god, "and the priests, mindful of the benefits of Osiris, desirous of gratifying the queen, and moved by the prospect of gain, carried out all the injunctions of Isis" (Frazer 424). *The Sound and the Fury*, Herbert Head, whom Caddy has met during her travels, pays homage to Quentin:

> Thanks I've heard a lot I guess your mother wont mind if I put the match behind the screen will she a lot about you Candace talked

about you all the time up there at the Licks I got pretty jealous I says to myself who is this Quentin anyway I must see what this animal looks like because I was hit pretty hard see soon as I saw the little girl I don't mind telling you it never occurred to me it was her brother she kept talking about she couldn't have talked about you any more if you'd been the only man in the world husband wouldn't have been it you won't change your mind and have a smoke" (133).

Frazer cites the lament of the sisters of Osiris: "they wailed, 'Come to thy house. O god On! Come to thy house, thou hast no foes. O fair youth, come to thy house, that thou mayst see me. I am thy sister, whom thou lovest; thou shalt not part from me" (425). The house: Sutpen's hundred, the Compson Mile, perfect squares, the one a smaller version of the other. Frazer speaks of the resurrection of Osiris:

The lamentations of the two sad sisters were not in vain. In pity for their sorrow the sun-god Ra sent down from heaven the jackal-headed god Anubis, who, with the aid of Isis and Nephthys, of Thoth and Horus, pieced together the broken body of the murdered god, swathed it in linen bandages, and observed all the other rites which the Egyptians were wont to perform over the bodies of the departed. Then Isis fanned the cold clay with her wings: Osiris revived, and thenceforth reigned as king over the dead in the other world. There he bore the titles of Lord of the Underworld, Lord of Eternity, Ruler of the Dead *(425)*.

Candace "was two months pregnant with another man's child, which regardless of what its sex would be she had already named Quentin after the brother whom they both (she and the brother) knew was already the same as dead" (SF Appendix 413). Or perhaps this is a function of the novel itself, preserving the life of Quentin, of Charles, of Thomas Sutpen, in that other world.

4. Dionysus. We have already described some of the mythic parallels between Dionysus and Wash Jones. Introducing Frazer's Dionysus adds a few more details:

a. "one of his titles was 'teeming' or bursting (as of sap or blossoms)" (Frazer 449). Jones lives on the wild bottom of the Tallahatchie, amid the densest profusion of vegetation.

b. "He is spoken of as himself doing the work of the husbandman: he is reported to have been the first to yoke oxen to the plough, which before had been dragged by hand alone" (Frazer *450)*. During the war Jones helps Judith by working in the fields, by ploughing the earth and growing a garden to feed her.

c. "Like other gods of vegetation Dionysus was believed to have died a violent death . . . for the treacherous Titans, their faces whitened with chalk, attacked him with knives while he was looking at himself in a mirror" (Frazer *450-51)*. Jones, having killed Sutpen, contemplates his own life. He is killed by Major De Spain and the posse, who come in the evening.

5. Demeter and Persephone. "The youthful Persephone, so runs the tale, was gathering *roses* and *lilies* , crocuses and violets, *hyacinths* and *narcissuses* in a lush meadow, when the earth gaped and Pluto, lord of the Dead, issuing from the abyss carried her off on his golden car to be his bride and queen in the gloomy and subterranean world." (Frazer *456,* emphasis mine). Persephone's mother, Demeter, goddess of the grain, who in mourning allowed the grain to whither, until Zeus intervened and ordered Pluto to relinquish his bride.

> The grim lord of the Dead smiled and obeyed, but before he sent back his queen to the upper air on a golden car, he gave her the seed of a pomegranate to eat, which insured that she would return to him. But Zeus stipulated that henceforth Persephone should spend two thirds of every year with her mother and the gods in the upper world and one third of the year with her husband in the nether world, from which she was to return year by year when the earth was gay with spring flowers. Gladly the daughter then returned to the sunshine, gladly her mother received her and fell upon her neck; and in her joy at recovering her lost one Demeter made the corn to sprout from the clods of the ploughed fields and all the broad earth to be heavy with leaves and blossoms (Frazer *457)*.

Rosa Coldfield sees her sister Ellen as a highly subverted form of Persephone, and Thomas Sutpen as Pluto. Ellen has no mother, only a younger sister; she returns only a few days a year, and these occasions are less than joyful. But the fact of awayness coincides strikingly from a passage in *Absalom:* "It was as though the sister whom I had never laid eyes on, who before I was born had vanished into the stronghold of an ogre or a djinn, was now to return through a dispensation of one day, to the world which she had quitted" (AA 23). *From Ritual to Romance* supplies the most relevant parallel for our purposes: the parallel between the Perceval legend and Quentin's journey to Sutpen's Hundred in *Absalom*. In this interstice, *Quentin* is Perceval, the young knight who undertakes the journey in *Quest* of the Grail; the Grail Castle being Sutpen's mansion, which lies in the middle of a barren and ruined land, the Waste Land, Sutpen's Hundred. The Fisher King, "fallen into a doleful sickness" (Weston 16), is like Henry, "the wasted yellow face with closed, almost transparent eyelids on the pillow, the wasted hands crossed on the breast as if he were already a corpse" (AA 373).

Weston distills from the numerous written versions of the Perceval legend two essential outcomes of the Quest: the successful cure of the Fisher King and restoration of the land, and the Failed Quest, which occurs after the hero views the Grail ritual, but fails to inquire into the purpose and meaning of it. Thus the land is not restored, and thus the king dies.

From a psychoanalytic perspective, the motif of the Waste Land might well serve as a metaphor for the condition of neurosis, and the Grail a metaphor for the Cure, the restoration to health. Thus the long process of telling and remembering can be interpreted as a quest, and the long telling of the buried life, of the Sutpen story, is Quentin's quest. And this quest is the failed Quest, for the king dies, the castle vanishes, and the land is left as badly off as before. But what is the question that Quentin has failed to ask? What is the meaning of the ritual; what is the source of the curse? This issue will stand behind our continued speculation, for awhile as a latent guide and governor.

II

As we have shown earlier, many critics are intuitively drawn the motif of the waste land as a metaphor for the psychological conditions which prevail in Faulkner's many novels, among these *Absalom*. But as we have seen also, the history of this metaphor reveals it as a vague and imprecise term. And if this term is to be used in critical discourse in such a way as to accommodate in even a small way the incredible richness and suggestiveness it in possibility contains, it is necessary to impose on it a disciplined definition. I will assert that the definition we seek lies within Brown's theory of the psychology of monetary wealth, that is, the erotic life of the body displaced from sexuality outward into external things, dead things, the symbols of excrement. In order to map out this position more fully, we will provide a series of citations from the concluding section of "Filthy Lucre" in *Life Against Death*

> The repudiation of the body does not and cannot alter the fact that life in the body is all we have, and the unconscious holds fast to the truth and never makes the repudiation; in the id, says Freud, there is nothing corresponding to the act of negation. Hence the net effect of the ego's repudiation of bodily life can only be the diversion of bodily Eros from its natural task of sustaining the life of the body to the unnatural task of constructing life-in-death for the body. Thus the morbid attempt to get away from the body can only result in a morbid fascination (erotic cathexis) in the death of the body. In the simple and true, because bodily, language of the unconscious, Eros can only be deflected from the life of the body only by being deflected onto the excremental function. In the true life of the body (which is also the life of the id) value can be detached from the body only by attaching value to the nonbodily excreta of the body, which are at the same time the dead matter produced by the body, and which incorporate the body's daily dying (293-94).

. . .

In the last analysis, the peculiar human fascination with excrement is the peculiar human fascination with death *(295)*.

. . .

Excrement is the dead life of the body, and as long as humanity prefers a dead life to living, so long as humanity is committed to treating as excrement not only its own body but the surrounding word of objects, reducing all to dead matter and inorganic magnitudes. Our much prized "objectivity" toward our own bodies, other persons, and the universe, all our calculating "rationality," is, from the psychoanalytical point of view, an ambivalent mixture of love and hate, and attitude appropriate to excrement only in an animal that has lost his own body and life (295).

. . .

The connection between sublimation, the death instinct, and excrement is not static, but subject to the dynamics of the neurosis which is human history. Culture originates in the denial of the life of the body, and the impossibility of denying life in the body is what makes all cultures unstable diffusions of life instinct and death instinct (297).

. . .

Sublimations are these negations of the body which simultaneously affirm it; and sublimations achieve this dialectical tour de force by the simple but basic mechanism of projecting the repressed body into things. The more the life of the body passes into things, the less life there is in the body, and at the same time the increasing accumulation of things represents an ever fuller articulation of the lost life of the body (297).

. . .

The transformation of life into death-in-life, which is the achievement of higher civilization, prepares mankind to accept death (298).

. . .

In Seri magic, excrement is literally aliment; but before we read them out of the roll of humanity, let us remember what happened to Midas (301).

. . .

This withdrawal of Eros hands over culture to the death instinct; and the inhuman, abstract, impersonal world which the death instinct creates progressively eliminates all possibility of the life of sublimated Eros, which we nostalgically so admire in the ancient Greeks. Thus the path of sublimation ends in its own self-refutation and sets the stage for its own abolition. At the same time this transformation of life into death-in-life is a victory for the reality-principle. The withdrawal of Eros from sublimation is the great disillusionment (303).

The term "waste land" is synonymous with "land of excrement." Hell can be neither fire nor ice, because fire and ice are often desired and loved by the body. Hell is excrement, that which the body utterly rejects, and which it finds utterly disgusting. The preceding chapters of this exercise have served nothing if not to demonstrate that *Absalom* indeed presents a waste land vision, provided that our definition of the term is appropriate. And an examination of the imagery of Eliot's poem affirms that this is the case. The poem's 434 lines utterly crystallize the entire pathology of the neurosis which is civilization, which is time, which is human history, religion, copulation, commerce, which is Jason Compson's sum total of human failures and Stephen Dedalus' nightmare of history from which he tries to awaken (Joyce *35).*

The poem's unified structure is a system of thematic groupings, and these groups are structured around the figures of life-in-death, which commence in its opening lines. These are the lines which signify the Fall into Division, the separation anxiety as a consciousness is thrust from the amniotic state, torn from the unconscious, that which is "covering! Earth in forgetful snow, feeding! A little life with dried tubers." *(5- 7),* awakening and growing in daylight, subject to division, drawing the primal boundaries: "Bin gar keine Russin, stamm' aus Lituaen, echt Deutsch" (12). A collective ego emerges, defined in relation to projected *others,* the arch-duke its representative, and Marie lies awake at night, afraid of what is repressed and buried in the unconsciousness, dreaming on the pages of a book. The civilized ego is constructed, locked in its prison and palace.

The prophetic question, "What are the roots that clutch, what branches grow/ Out of this stony rubbish?" (19-20); the stony rubbish of the Waste Land, the stones of the Unreal City, the city sublime, the burnished throne, the marble, glass, jewels, vials of ivory, the room cluttered with excremental symbols, the garbage along the Thames, the currants of Mr. Eugenides, the Young Man Carbuncular, the drowned sailor whose eyes are pearls, all stony rubbish, all the setting for "the agony in stony places" (324), the agony suffered by the poem's pageant of voices, which resemble Faulkner's haunted narrators who are unable to live, unable to die, each voice a figure of life-in-death. The Hyacinth Girl: "I was neither/ Living nor dead, and I knew nothing" (39-40), and Madame Sosostris' "Crowds of people, walking around in a ring" *(56),* are examples of civilization's Faustian discontents, here patterned here like Dante's circular city in Hell, each one a citizen of the Unreal City, part of this scene: "A crowd flowed over London Bridge, so many. I had not thought death had undone so many" (62- 63); each one is the corpse planted in the garden (71). Life and death are fused in a malevolent paradox haunting a consciousness which is psychologically incapable of either living or dying, a consciousness which is like a series of dreams emanating from the 120 original fantasy of return to the maternal womb, "feeding! A little life with dried tubers" (6-7); from which the primal sense of *We* individuates, through the projections of *Us* and *Them* , into the modern sense of *I* . Now, amid the cluttered interior, the room of the burnished throne, the room of the aristocrat with its myriad symbols of wealth and waste, the drama of fear resolves into the same dream. Fear is the shadow that falls between, the anxiety and sense of the uncanny that accompanies the return of the repressed. The shadow under the red rock: "fear in a handful of dust" (30), death and excrement combined in a single figure. The shadow falls along the boundary projected between Us and Them, a boundary held with armies and the reality of total war: 'you who were with me in the ships of Mylae!"

(70); "murmur of maternal lamentation! Who are those hooded hordes swarming! Over endless plains, stumbling in cracked earth" (368-70). The shadow is "the third who always walks beside you" (360), and "the wind under the door" (118). Here in the drama of two voices, one female and speaking and filled with anxiety, the repressed lurking in some unspeakable form, the second voice inward, Urizenic: "What are you thinking of, what thinking? What?! 'I never know what you are thinking. Think." (113-14), answered with a figure of hell: "I think we are in rat's alley! Where the dead men lost their bones (115-16). This is what the returning repressed is:

> Do
> you know nothing? Do you see nothing? Do you remember
> 'Nothing
> I remember
> Those are pearls that were his eyes.
> 'Are you alive or not? Is there nothing in your head?' (121- 26).

This scene figures an epiphany of life-in-death, alluding to 1) 'The Fire Sermon":

> But at my back in a cold blast I hear
> The rattle of bones, and a chuckle spread
> from ear to ear.
>
> A rat crept softly, through the vegetation
> Dragging its slimy belly on the bank.
> While I was fishing in the dull canal
> On a winter evening round behind the gashouse
> Musing on the king my brother's wreck
> And on the king my father's death before him (185-92)

and 2) "Death by Water": "Phlebas the Phoenician, a fortnight dead! Forgot the cry of gulls, and the deep sea swell! And the profit and loss" (312-14). Between these lies the Unreal City (207) and its system of money which ravages it: upon the stage of late capitalism the Primal Scene is enacted, viewed by the androgynous spectator, the castrated child, Tiresias. What the child is fascinated with is not two impassioned bodies lost in the joy of each other, but two persons, actors on a socioeconomic stage, a Typist and a House Agent's Clerk. They *enact* (244) the ritual of eating, in which excrement is aliment, because the "food in tins" (223) undoubtedly tastes like *shit*. The meal is the *prologue* to the *enactment* of coitus, which here is a highly genitalized ritual, which lacks all the freedom of play, all pleasure, even the working advantage of procreation: "she is bored and tired" (236); "His vanity requires no response! And makes a welcome of indifference" (241-42), and finally, "Her brain allows one half-formed thought to pass:! 'Well now that's done: and I'm glad it's over" *(25 1-52)*.

The logical extension of the *enactment* falls in the voices of the prostitutes which follow: the life of the body, with all its marvelous ability to love and give life, is reduced to a quick and meaningless act which is the transaction of the coin; sexuality is reduced to its market value.

The Unreal City is the city in Time, "where Saint Mary Woolnoth kept the hours! With a dead sound on the final stroke of nine (67-68). The consciousness ends out in a discontent, a sense of rush, "HURRY UP PLEASE ITS TIME" (141), the voice of the pubkeeper speaking to the unconsciousness that the very prescence of time impels the sense of hurry; the logical formula for this can be stated: "Time, therefore Hurry Up." The final stroke of nine: a dead sound, impelling the hurrying crowd in hell, in London, the hour of death in a thousand offices where the working day begins, leaving those who have accumulated wealth and therefore leisure and freedom from this to ask

> What shall we do tomorrow
> 'Whatever shall we do?'
> The hot water at ten,
> and if it rains, a closed car at four. (133-36)

In the economic nightmare which ravages the Waste Land, however, time imposes no limits. The value of money lies in the unconscious; in the unconscious there is no time, and eternal life is invested in coin and stone. Therefore, in Eliot, the history of business occupies a single moment, in which British late capitalism, Renaissance-era mercantilism, and the archaic trade of the Eastern Mediterranean are interfused. Thus, the Symrna merchant appears in London, the death of the Phoenician is foretold by a modern European medium, an Englishman is recognized in London as a veteran of the Punic Wars, Tiresias the Theban views the seduction of one whose role was created in the course of turn-of-the-century technology. The throne room in "A Game of Chess" is a repository of all centuries of accumulated wealth, with its Cupids and paintings of classical legends, a modern building which was built on the symbolic level by the ancient Greeks and occupied continuously through the Roman Empire and into modern times. The Waste Land is haunted by a fear of the uncanny, of things repressed returning in a new and uglier form, though each new occurrence is a repetition of an archetypal event. Thus the rape of Philomel forms the archetypal basis for the seduction of the typist. This anxiety is intensified in the throne room, purified into a fear of "the wind under the door" (118).

The Unreal City is a city of temples in which time and money repose: "Saint Mary Woolnoth kept the hours" (67); "the walls! Of Magnus Martyr hold! Inexplicable splendor of Ionian white and gold" (263-65). Time is visible; the names of streets contain history: King William (66) and Queen Victoria (258), monarchs of the past, representatives of the National Body, the collective of the dead, lords of the ancestors who rule the underworld and constitute a visible presence among the living. As the weight of time increases, the sacrifice demanded of the living intensifies. A metaphor for this process is the series of references to Frazerian rites for restoring vegetation: "That corpse you planted last year in your garden, /'Has it begun to sprout? Will it bloom again this year" (71-72); "White bodies naked on the low damp ground" (193); the opening stanza of "What the Thunder Said": all scenes of human sacrifice.

The logical outcome of the accumulation of repressed guilt is apocalypse. When the burden of the repressed becomes too great for the unconscious to bear, the mechanism of repression fails, and sublimated filth is revealed as literal filth. In the Unreal City, the human psyche is forced to conform to abstract models of its own forging, increasingly becoming alienated from its natural life, locked into a personhood in which possibilities become increasingly diminished. This is the sacrifice performed in the temples of the Unreal City; its prototype is human sacrifice of the ritual paganism which stands behind the culture of modern Europe, and all of history spanning this dark past and even darker present is contained in the stones of Mary Woolnoth and London Bridge. Civilization is a nightmare; the apocalypse is an awakening.

The final section of *The Waste Land* presents the figures of a final conflagration, in which the conditions of the Unreal City are represented in absolute terms. The stones of the city here are "mountains of rock without water" (334), which have consumed the sacrifice. Death lingers on these stones, "Dead mountains of carious teeth that cannot spit" (339). Like the city, the mountains are inhabited by the unfriendly and wretched: "red sullen faces sneer and snarl! from doors of mudcracked houses." *(344-45)*. Images of armies ['hooded hordes swarming! Over endless plains, stumbling in cracked earth" (369-70)], of hell, lead logically and fluidly into the fall of the City:

> Cracks and reforms and bursts in the violet air
> Falling Towers
> Jerusalem Athens Alexandria
> Vienna London
> Unreal (373-77).

The City is at all times and all places a pure psychological condition. It is a city of cathedrals, dislocated in the pure space of apocalypse: "Upside down in air were towers! Tolling reminiscent bells that kept the hours! And voices singing out of empty cisterns and exhausted wells (383-85). The Waste Land is a necropolis: "over the tumbled graves, about the chapel! There is the empty chapel, only the wind's home" (388-89)

The Thunder speaks in figures of judgment: the life of the body, real life, "blood shaking my heart" (403) is set over and against the unreal life, which is death, recorded "in our obituaries" (407), "or under seals broken by the lean solicitor" (409). The choice between real life and life-in-death is reformulated in the figure of the key and the prison, and the lines "Only at nightfall, aetherial rumors! Revive for a moment a broken Coriolanus" (416-17), find their Faulknerian analog in the character of Reverend Hightower in *Light in August* , who waits each evening for his ghostly confederate ancestors to come thundering on horses down the empty street.

Eliot's poem *The Waste Land* ends in the eschatological question. Will the rain come? Will the dead land be restored? Does the King fishing by the river await his redemption? or will he remain forever in the land of fallen towers? The question is left undecidable: neither hope not complete despair provide certain options, while both remain ambiguous possibilities.

III

In the Faulknerian Waste Land of *Absalom, Absalom!,* the retelling of the tale of ancestors can be read as a psychoanalytic quest, a search through the ruins of the past for the grail that is the cure, that can restore Rosa and Quentin and Clytie and Henry to true life. It is an eschatological quest for the dawn breaking through the night of the psyche, for the fulfillment of hope.

For Norman O. Brown, the eschatological question is the central problem in philosophy; the psychoanalytic critique of history is also a quest for redemption, and exploration of the possibility of fulfillment. Nietzsche, likewise, near the conclusion of *The Birth of Tragedy,* in a moment of exaltation proclaims his highest hope:

> "indeed, my friends, believe with me in this Dionysian life and in the rebirth of tragedy! Socratic man has run his course; crown your heads with ivy, seize the thyrsus, and do not be surprised if the tiger and panther lie down and caress your feet! Dare to lead the life of tragic man, and you will be redeemed" (124).

This idea is expressed more fully in *Thus Spoke Zarathustra* , in the figure of the Overman: "The Overman is the meaning of the earth What does your body proclaim of your soul? Is not your soul poverty and filth and wretched contentment? "Verily, a polluted stream is man. One must be a sea to be able to receive a polluted stream without becoming unclean. Behold, I teach you the Overman: he is this sea; in him your great contempt can go under" (125). Brown's psychoanalytic analog to the Overman is the coming of the Dionysian ego, an ego strong enough to both live and die, to live more fully by accepting the unity of life and death: Brown views this as a process of evolution:

> With such a transfigured body the human soul can be reconciled, and the human ego become once more what it was designed to be in the first place, a body-ego and the surface of the body, sensing that communication between body and body which is life. But the path to that ultimate reunification of ego and body is not a dissolution of but a strengthening of the human ego. The human ego would have to become strong enough to die; and strong enough to set aside guilt. Archaic consciousness was strong enough to set aside guilt; Christian consciousness is strong enough to recognize the debt is so great only God can redeem it; modern secular Faustian man is strong enough to live with irredeemable damnation; full psychoanalytical consciousness would be strong enough to cancel the debt by deriving it from infantile fantasy (LD 292).

By broadening the scope of our interpretation of *Absalom,* through the expansion of our analogy to include the Waste Land, we have brought our exercise to its crisis, a crisis which Christine de Montauzon regards as inevitable:

> *Absalom* opens a vast testing field for accommodations only to abort them in the maze of the text itself.

> The task is to show how *Absalom* responds to and ultimately defeats any and all critical efforts at interpretive closure.

> Reading *Absalom* and writing about this reading dramatize a crisis in the making of sense. Both the novel and this thesis show involve the difficult gestation of meaning in the face of a fragmented and evanescent reality. They make us experience that Meaning as absolute Presence of a final hidden Totality that may exist only in our Desire for it: in *Absalom* , we encounter the making of sense as the functional freeplay of diverse uncompletable accommodations. In this novel, Meaning becomes Experience and no longer Transcendence (xiii-xv).

The eschatological problem is the point of the crisis in the Brownian interpretation of Faulkner. If the psychoanalytic critique of history is to be viewed as a myth which the Faulknerian text parallels, then the eschatological problem is the point at which the parallel is subverted. The novel presents few alternatives to the sublimation of Sutpen and Rosa, and a brief review of these indicates that none of them develop into a viable eschatology.

Charles Bon is the living symbol of the burden of Sutpen guilt, a man who, although impaled on the distinctions of race and family, nevertheless manages to continue living, to continue as a functioning ego. In his letter to Judith, he describes a philosophy of the body: "*it really does not become inured to hardship and privation; it is only the mind, the gross omnivorous carrion-heavy soul which becomes inured; the body itself, thank God, never reconciled from the old soft feel of soap and clean linen and something between the sole of the foot and the earth to distinguish it from the foot of a beast."* (130). Bon concludes, 'We have waited long enough* " (131). He understands that the past of his country in *1865* has died, and the life of the body is all that he and Judith have, and he is prepared for them both to live this life in living marriage. Henry, through his own heroic effort, has suspended the incest taboo, and the marriage of brother and sister can take place, and perhaps produce a new order. But Henry cannot accept this in the face of the revelation of Bon's negro ancestry; and all hope of a better, fuller life dies with the killing of Bon.

Wash Jones, as we have seen, experiences in the final hours of his life a Dionysian awareness. But this produces no strengthening of his ego, rather its dissolution.

Judith works hard after the war in the service of life, burying the dead and nurturing the living. She cares for Etienne Bon, giving him an opportunity to leave his black past behind and lead a new life as a free man. But he rejects this chance, and both he and Judith die of fever without having finally brought renewal to the Waste Land.

Which leaves only Quentin's quest for the grail as a possible avenue of fulfillment. But what is this grail? There can be no doubt that the answer to this lies in the problem of racism, which, as Eric Sundquist demonstrates, is the central fact which structures the peculiar neurosis from which the South as a whole suffers. The heart of the problem lies in the practice on the part of whites to view blacks as less than human, as animals, and at the same time to take them as sexual partners. Thus the greatest fear of the white Southerner deconstructs into two features: the fear that a white woman will conceive a child by a black man, a child which would be half human and half something else, and also the fear of discovering a black ancestor in one's genealogy, and thus to find oneself a "nigger" whose skin is white.

Jim Bond, the mulatto idiot, scion of the Sutpen ascendency and heir to the estate, is the living embodiment of this fear which has a stranglehold on the imagination of a whole society. To confront Jim Bond is to face and possibly overcome one's own deepest fear. This is the opportunity Quentin receives at Sutpen's Hundred, which might involve the accomplishment of an equilibrium which Derrida describes as follows:

> At other times the equilibrium is established in a static manner, through a play of forces precisely pitted against each other, whose total balance amounts to the euphoria of a 'suspension.' It is thus that Mallarmé himself indeed envisioned the internal reality of a poem and the ideal architecture of the objects the poem must reorder within itself: grottos, diamonds, spider webs, rose windows, shells, kiosks, all stand as so many images which translate the search for a total correlation of nature with itself, a *perfect equalization of all things.* The mind or spirit then becomes the keystone of this architecture, functioning as the absolute center through which everything communicates, balances out, and is neutralized (Mallarmé adds 'is annulled *(Dissemination* 247)

Since the problem of racism is a problem within the imagination, then a solution would no doubt be imaginative as well. This balancing out, or in Brownian terms, canceling the debt, is what the narration created by Quentin and Shreve must accomplish. It must create an imaginative space within which all things are equalized, including Black and White, truly a task for the Dionysian Ego. The annulment of a debt is precisely the figure Shreve uses in expressing the following:

> So it took Charles Bon and his mother to get rid of old Tom, and Charles Bon and the Octoroon to get rid of Judith, and Charles

Bon arid Clytie to get rid of Henry; and Charles Bon's mother and Charles Bon's grandmother got rid of Charles Bon. So it takes two niggers to get rid of one Sutpen, dont it? Which is all right, it's fine; it clears the whole ledger, you can tear all the pages out and burn them, except for one thing. And do you know what that is?... You've got one nigger left. One nigger Sutpen left. Of course you can't catch him and you don't even always see him and you will never be able to use him. But you've got him there still. You hear him at night sometimes. Don't you? (AA 377-78).

The whole situation is reduced to the crystal of the nightmare. Faulkner's Perceval has failed to ask the appropriate question concerning the Grail, and the Castle has vanished, and the hand of death remains upon the land. And Quentin, who has failed to ask the meaning of all he has heard and seen, lies awake in the dark, horrified by the thought of Jim Bond ruling the world and becoming the father of the whole white race of which he can no longer be sure of membership. The quest for renewal has failed, and Quentin is one step closer it his coming suicide.

IV

The reader, then, is the only field in which the Dionysian Ego may yet be realized. In facing a novel in which the traditional critical concepts of plot and character have become utterly problematic, a novel in which all attempts to arrive at a totalized understanding are systematically subverted, it is necessary for the mind to relinquish the very need for an Apollonian understanding, that is, a comprehensive critical document, and work solely within that condition of fluid ambiguity within which thought occurs. This requires the development of an intellectual discipline which utterly departs from the western tradition which Nietzsche calls Socratism, that is, logocentrism, or the ideal of a truth which is knowable through reason. This exercise is a continuation of this quest, which has been the task of Faulkner criticism form Irwin on, and, as an attempt to respond to a fluid text with a group of other texts fluidly integrated, reflects the pressures of this in finding its form. It is my hope and I believe it is the hope of others who have undertaken these explorations that interpreting Faulkner in ways such as this will allow or compel the reader to confront within himself his or her own nightmare. It is only in this way that *Absalom, Absalom!* though it describes only the neurosis of man, the Waste Land, may yet form an element in that partnership which engenders the Overman. It is the reader who is compelled to confront himself through the text, to confront those issues which affect us most deeply: will we be saved from our own weaponry, our atomic bomb which so resembles the burst of Sutpen's innocence on the empty plain of his vision, leaving its monument, death, the destroyer of worlds?

Will we be able to end Apartheid in South Africa, or the similar problems in Ireland and the Middle East? Or resolve the racial dilemma which continues to plague the U.S.? That is, will we ever be able to heal the division within the House divided?

And what of the problem of Real Estate, the single vision which promotes Property and the selling of the land, which destroys the forests of this planet for plantations so vast and so environmentally destructive that they destroy the air and threaten the very biosphere?

These problems are the logical symptoms of the same human neurosis which structures Faulkner's world, a certain way of thinking and interpreting reality, which it is clear that we must overcome. But the divisions within collective man have their analog and origin in the divisions within the individual, and it is these which we must confront as humans and therefore as reader and critic also. The violence of this confrontation enables each of us to encounter the possibility of generating new paradigms which would enable us to overcome our present difficulties, an accomplishment which, as we have seen, involves the overcoming of man himself. To experience revolution as a merely personal epiphany, is only to step from the neurosis of culture into a moral vacuum, which others would perceive as madness, while business goes on as usual all around. Revolution must therefore be collective. And yet there must be some avant garde who can exploit these breaks in the facade of what is believed.

Snead remarks:

That there is a possibility for revolution in language, and perhaps an abrupt one, is the major premise of Faulkner, particularly in his novels between 1929 and 1940 . . . While Joyce, Beckett, Pound, and Eliot were thematizing and otherwise exploiting at this time the estrangement of Signifier from signified, Faulkner had traced in his "county' and "country" the social ramifications of what other writers thought largely and aesthetic quandary. Man's separation from his fellow men and labor, as Faulkner saw, is an inevitable result of the attempt to overlook the economic factors that underpin semiotic discrimination. (134-35).

Revolution: language must contain within itself the possibility of a paradigm which, by bursting all at once into the collective consciousness, will engender the instantaneous dissolution of the whole Apollonian structure of reality, and the spontaneous undoing of history. The logical outcome of such an event would be the abandonment of all governments, all wars, and all institutional business as we know it. The soldier would wonder why he still holds the gun; the banker would find his office and his reasons for being there and doing what he does utterly strange. This is the revolution which Faulkner does not predict, yet clearly points to, and demonstrates the need for: when we quite literally forget what we are fighting over, and why we wanted the profit from the sale, and find ourselves suddenly and joyously within a new reality which is wholly unforeseen.

Works Cited

Adams, Richard P. *Faulkner: Myth and Motion*. Princeton: Princeton U.P., 1968.

Brooks, Cleanth. *The Well Wrought Urn*. New York: Harcourt, Brace & World, 1947.

- - *William Faulkner: The Yoknapatawpha Country*. New Haven: Yale U.P., 1968.

Brown, Norman 0. *Life Against Death: The Psychoanalytical Meaning of History*. New York: Random House, 1959.

- - *Love's Body*. New York: Random House, 1966.

Blotner, Joseph. *William Faulkner: A Biography*. One Volume Edition. New York: Random House, 1974.

Derrida, Jacques. *Dissemination*. Trans. Barbara Johnson. Chicago: U. of Chicago P., 1981.

- - *La dissemination*. Paris: Editions du Seuil, 1972.

Dickerson, Mary Jane. "'As I Lay Dying' and 'The Waste Land': Some Relationships." *Mississippi Quarterly* Summer 1964: 129-35.

Eliot, T.S. *Collected Poems* 1909-1962. New York: Harcourt, Brace & World, 1963. "The Waste Land": 51-76. "The Hollow Men": 77-82.

- - "Ulysses, Order, and Myth." *Dial* November 1923: 480-83.

Fasel, Ida. "A 'Conversation' Between Faulkner and Eliot." *Mississippi Quarterly* Fall 1967: 195-206.

Faulkner, William. *Absalom, Absalom!*. New York: Modern Library, 1964.

- - *The Sound and the Fury*. New York: Random House, 1954.

- - *Light in August.* New York: Random House, 1972.

- - *Go Down, Moses.* New York: Random House, 1973.

- - "A Rose for Emily." Elizabeth McMahon, Susan Day, Robert Frank, eds. *Literature and the Writing Process.* New York: MacMillan, 1986: 253-59.

Frazer, Sir James George. *The Golden Bough: A Study in Magic and Religion.* One Volume, Abridged Edition. New York: MacMillan, 1951.

Freud, Sigmund. "Beyond the Pleasure Principle." *The Complete Psychological Works of Sigmund Freud.* Vol. XVIII, 7-64. London: Hogarth, 1957. 138

Hopkins, Gerard Manley. "The Caged Skylark." Ed. W.H. Gardner. *Poems and Prose of Gerard Manley Hopkins.* Harmondsmith, Middlesex, England: Penguin, 1978: 31-32.

Irwin, John T. *Doubling and Incest/Repetition and Revenge.* Baltimore: Johns Hopkins U.P., 1975.

Jaynes, Julian. *The Origin of Consciousness in the Breakdown of the Bicameral Mind.* Boston: Houghton Mifflin, 1976.

Joyce, James. *Ulysses.* New York: Modern Library, 1934: 35.

Jung, C.G. "The Relations Between the Ego and the Unconscious." *Two Essays on Analytical Psychology.* Trans. R.F.C. Hull. Cleveland: World Publishing, 1956.

Kayman, Martin. *The Modernism of Ezra Pound: The Science of Poetry.* London: MacMillan, 1986.

Matthews, John T. *The Play of Faulkner's Language.* Baltimore: Johns Hopkins U.P., 1983.

de Montauzon, Christine. *Faulkner's Absalom, Absalom! and Interpretability: The Inexplicable Unseen.* Berne: Peter Lang, 1985. 139

Newman, Peter C. "The Hudson's Bay Company: Canada's Fur Trading Empire." *National Geographic,* August 1987: 192-229.

Nietzsche, Friedrich. *The Birth of Tragedy and The Geneology of Morals.* Trans. Francis Golffing. Garden City, N.Y.: Doubleday, 1956.

- - "Twilight of the Idols." *The Portable Nietzsche.* Trans. Walter Kaufman. New York: Viking, 1954: 463-563.

- - "Thus Spoke Zarathustra." Trans. Kaufman: 103-439.

Poirier, Richard. "'Strange Gods' in Jefferson, Mississippi: Analysis of *Absalom, Absalom!*" *William Faulkner's* Absalom, Absalom!: *A Critical Casebook.* Ed. Elisabeth Muhlenfeld. New York: Garland, 1984.

Rollyson, Carl. *Uses of the Past in the Novels of William Faulkner.* Ann Arbor: U.M.I. Research Press, 1984.

Slabey, Robert M. "Faulkner's 'Waste Land' Vision in *Absalom, Absalom!*" *Mississippi Quarterly* Summer 1961: 153-161. Snead, James A. *Figures of Division.* New York: Methuen, 1986.

Robin, Régine. "Absalom, Absalom!" Ed. Viola Sachs. *Le Blanc et Le Noir Chez Melville et Faulkner.* Paris: Mouton, 1974: 67-129. 140

Stevens, Wallace. "Sunday Morning." *The Collected Poems of Wallace Stevens.* New York: Knopf, 1955: 66-70.

Sundquist, Eric J. *Faulkner: The House Divided.* Baltimore: Johns Hopkins U.P., 1983. Volpe, Edward. *A Reader's Guide to William Faulkner.* London: Thames and Hudson, 1964.

Wadlington, Warwick. *Reading Faulknerian Tragedy.* Ithaca: Cornell U.P., 1987.

Weston, Miss Jessie L. *From Ritual to Romance.* Garden City, N.Y.: Doubleday, 1957.

Abbreviations

Works by Norman 0. Brown:

ID *Life Against Death*
LB *Love's Body*

Works by T. S. Eliot:

HM "The Hollow Men"
WL "The Waste Land"

Works by William Faulkner:

AA *Absalom, Absalom!*
SF *The Sound and the Fury*
LA *Light in August*
GDM *Go Down, Moses*

Works by Friedrich Nietzsche:

BT "The Birth of Tragedy"
GM "The Genealogy of Morals"
TI "Twilight of the Idols"
Z "Thus Spoke Zarathustra"